Frances Farrer is a writer, broadcaster and journalist who specialises in the subject of children and education. She was on the staff of *The Times Educational Supplement* for many years and is now a regular freelance contributor to it. Her children's stories have been broadcast on Radio 4, her plays for children have played to capacity audiences at the Edinburgh Festival Fringe and she has produced three arts festivals for children on London's South Bank.

At the time of writing the introduction to this book, Neil Hawkes was the headmaster of West Kidlington Primary School, Oxfordshire, where the positive values programme evolved and was put into practice. Since then he has been appointed by the Oxfordshire Education Authority with a comprehensive brief that includes developing a values-based approach to teaching and learning in schools. He is also an international consultant for values education and speacks for UNICEF and UNESCO.

A Quiet Revolution

Encouraging positive values in our children

Frances Farrer

With an introduction by Neil Hawkes

RIDER

LONDON • SYDNEY • AUCKLAND • JOHANNESBURG

1 3 5 7 9 10 8 6 4 2

First published in 2000 by Rider,
an imprint of Ebury Press, Random House,
20 Vauxhall Bridge Road, London SW1V 2SA
www.randomhouse.co.uk

Random House Australia (Pty) Limited
20 Alfred Street, Milsons Point, Sydney,
New South Wales 2061, Australia

Random House New Zealand Limited
18 Poland Road, Glenfield,
Auckland 10, New Zealand

Random House South Africa (Pty) Limited
Endulini, 5A Jubilee Road,
Parktown 2193, South Africa

The Random House Group Limited Reg. No. 954009

Papers used by Rider are natural, recyclable products made from
wood grown in sustainable forests.

Printed and bound in Great Britain by CPD Wales

A CIP catalogue record for this book
is available from the British Library

ISBN 0-7126-0577-0

'We are all meant to shine, as children do … And as we let our own light shine, we unconsciously give other people permission to do the same. And as we're liberated from our own fear, our presence automatically liberates others.'

Nelson Mandela

VALUES FOR LIVING

quality

unity

peace

happiness

hope

patience

caring

humility

simplicity

trust

freedom

co-operation

understanding

honesty

appreciation

courage

love

friendship

thoughtfulness

tolerance

responsibility

respect

Contents

Acknowledgements

This book would have been impossible without the help and co-operation of a great many people, and I wish to thank especially:

Neil Hawkes, who does not take the credit he deserves for this beautiful work.

Everyone at West Kidlington Primary School: all the teachers, all the general staff especially Angie Gardiner, Dianne Byford and Sue Lobban, the dinner ladies and Alex, all the children who gave interviews, the visitors who were inspired by it and said so and, above all, the spirit, joy, fun and aspiration of the children.

Brahma Kumaris for the inspiration of the positive words, the silent reflection, the emphasis on peacefulness.

Judith Kendra at Rider Books for being so in tune with it; and Juliet McKenna for the title.

My father, who backed me and enjoyed hearing about it; my mother, who taught me storytelling and loved little children.

Everyone who was encouraging and gave their good support when I was flagging.

Year groups are referred to throughout this book. Each year group relates to a specific age, and these are:

Key Stage 1 (otherwise known as Infants)
Year One: five- to six-year-old children
Year Two: six- to seven-year-old children

Key Stage 2 (otherwise known as Juniors)
Year Three: seven- to eight-year-old children
Year Four: eight- to nine-year-old children
Year Five: nine- to ten-year-old children
Year Six: ten- to eleven-year-old children

Preface

As you walk through the foyer of West Kidlington School the feeling of harmony is as powerful as the light that floods in through the glass roof. A child stops to ask if you need directions, then goes on his way. At reception they discover your purpose, set it in motion, and offer you a cup of tea. Your welcome is calm, businesslike and hospitable.

It is tempting to describe this state primary school in a dormitory village not far north of the ancient university city of Oxford as the other side of a particular Looking Glass where everything is quiet and orderly, where the children are hard-working, positive and funny, where there is no discord, and where any distress is swiftly put right.

None of this happens by chance. The school is working its transformations through a programme of positive values and the constant, gentle encouragement of positive qualities within every child. Each morning at assembly there are a couple of minutes' silent reflection on the month's chosen word, which might be honesty, truthfulness or respect. The concepts were chosen by the staff and are carried through into lessons. Honesty might be considered in a history or reading class, truthfulness in storytelling. Concepts apply equally to the staff: adults must be respectful during the month of respect and the head teacher will hold a door open for a six-year-old, whatever the current word. The parents are kept informed and most of them wholeheartedly support this work.

West Kidlington children are polite and centred and because their confidence comes from within it does not take the form of showing-off, although as they are encouraged to take delight in their work they will often show it to you. They know who they are and they know that they are valuable, so there is no need for display. They speak easily to adults, known and unknown, and to all their schoolmates of whatever age. They always give the time of day to visitors.

The older children take part in complex values discussions, which are remarkable as much for the frankness with which they talk about their confusions and struggles as for the clarity with which they work through the consequences of their actions and the possible alternatives. Younger children engage in a simpler version of this exercise and consider moral questions of surprising complexity.

The development of such clarity of mind naturally affects the academic effort and West Kidlington scores high in the national league tables of attainment. Even the school inspectors' reports praise the atmosphere in the school and the fine quality of the children. That this intangible effort is perceived by the government body designed to monitor only test results is further evidence of its strength. The inspectors themselves noted that the encouragement of values benefits the academic work.

My first encounter with the school followed a letter from the head teacher, Neil Hawkes, to the *Times Educational Supplement,* which led to me writing an article for the *TES* about the school assemblies and another about the value discussions. Later still I wrote a piece about the entire phenomenon for the *Independent.* With increasing contact I was increasingly impressed. Here was a profound effort being made, not in a rarefied environment, but within the context of what might be called an ordinary school, a state primary in a somewhat disadvantaged suburb.

This book has come about because of the great confusion outside, confusion about values, confusion about objectives, confusion about what to teach and how to teach it, and confusion about what children need to equip them for what promises to be a period of great change and instability. It is intended for parents and teachers but it may inspire others simply to see how much can be done in a day-to-day context if you set your mind to it.

The curiosity of the wider world to know more about this exciting work is growing fast, and Neil Hawkes is in demand to speak about it in all parts of the globe. He has spoken often in the USA, also in Scandinavia, Germany, Greece and other parts of Europe. Speaking engagements in recent months have included a Unicef conference for Arab educationists and ministers; lectures in Singapore, Malaysia and Israel; and many more in Oxfordshire, London and different parts of Great Britain.

The story of West Kidlington School combines theory with practice, aspiration with hands-on effort. I believe it is a beacon in a world at sea.

Frances Farrer

CHAPTER 1

The Road to West Kidlington

Neil Hawkes

*At the heart of a successful school is a commitment by the
school community to a clearly articulated set of values,
which enables it to strive for excellence.*

W HEN I TOOK UP MY fiRST TEACHING POST AT THE AGE OF 22
I was an idealist with a wish to be of use in the world. I had
all the fire and energy that comes from cherishing a positive
objective and from having had the immense good fortune to do my teaching
practices with inspiring, exciting teachers. These wonderful people had
shown me by example how much could be achieved in a classroom not
only in the mechanics of teaching subject disciplines but also in valuing
and strengthening the children.

Among my professional mentors when I was training was Timothy
Douglas. I spent a whole term with him, happily observing the method and
the man. Timothy took infinite trouble with everyone in the school: staff,
children, student teachers and me, and, in an era when school curricula
were determined by the local authority and the particular skills of their staff
I was impressed by the richness and variety he brought to his teaching. He
was able ensure that each child had access to the curriculum in a way
that was appropriate to his or her needs. Another of Timothy's excellent
qualities was that he would give an extraordinary amount of his own time
to talk to individual teachers and help their development. He created an
easy, friendly, relaxed and purposeful atmosphere in his school. During the

morning break he would play games with the children and at lunchtime he would ask them questions that were engaging and constructive. Both staff and pupils were enjoying learning: learning was an exciting journey that we made together. My external examiner, Harold Loukes from Oxford University, impressed upon me that I had had an outstanding experience in this small school and that it would be with me throughout my career.

In this nourishing situation I learned some vital things about values in teaching. I learned that forming a meaningful personal relationship with each child in my class was essential if they were to make good progress, since good relationships open the door to high self-esteem and the determination to please not only the teacher but also yourself. I learned that pupils deserve the very best of the teacher in terms of curriculum provision and commitment. Second best has no place! I learned that the quality of the teacher as a person is the most significant aspect of their teaching since the teacher is a most important role model for the child. I learned also that the disposition of the teacher has an enormous effect on the development and learning of the pupil. Lastly, I saw that each child brings values to the school based on experience at home and in the local community. This was to prove tremendously useful later when I began to look at ways of harmonising and unifying the human values work within my own schools.

Another hero of my early development was my personal tutor, Michael Oldfield; an educational philosopher and an inspiring man who was confined to a wheelchair after an early bout of polio. Perhaps it is a little obvious to say that people who have survived serious illness have a different depth of understanding, but whatever the cause, Michael was a brilliant teacher whose great quality was nurturing individuals by making them believe in their own ability. He exemplified the determination to succeed and make the most of his life despite his circumstances. His seminars were unique. He encouraged the growth of learning and understanding through the process of philosophy, valued everyone's contribution, never put anyone down for their remarks.

During my time with him I grew in confidence as I learned to present my own views and opinions. I learned that when working with a group of students I should make them feel important, and show them that their opinions counted. At the same time I saw that I should use humour in the classroom, and I saw that since pupils enjoy the chance of meeting adults at different levels I should not be afraid of revealing different aspects of myself. It is when children feel confident with you that they do their best work, and confidence is based on mutual respect.

Giving respect and having good manners are critically important because they enable people to be relaxed and open. Good manners had been a much earlier lesson for me, this time from my marvellous grandmother, another strong influence. In many ways she was a Victorian, believing in the good order of society and the importance of helping others less fortunate than you – although she was not a wealthy person. She taught me to show interest in others and respect for them. It was part of her creed that it is better to talk to people about themselves and their lives than to prattle on about yourself and your own concerns. Because of her I have tried to be open to the influence of people whose lives and thoughts seemed important and to learn from them. I believe the attempt to improve oneself is a lifelong effort that doesn't end with a diploma but continues indefinitely, and if we can bring the habit of observation and reflection into the lives of the children we teach we will have done them an invaluable service.

During my own schooldays I had a strong interest in drama as a way of discussing the human condition and expressing the character from the inside to the outside. In this I was again incredibly lucky in having a teacher who brought before me all the major works of Shakespeare, that profound observer of human psychology and behaviour. By the time I started teaching I had the germ of an idea about wholeness. Already it seemed to me that education should mean the entire child and not simply the programming by adults of facts and ideas into the developing brain for reproduction in an examination room.

I saw that children have to learn how to *be* in the world, how to deal with complex situations, how to observe and respond, and I believed that it was essential for them to do this from a position of strength and self-respect. I believed that such a desirable state was achievable by encouragement and that school should be the place for all this to be set in motion. That the strength of the individual is inherent but needs to be nurtured seems to me axiomatic. How many success stories begin with trials and difficulties in childhood overcome with the help of even just one supportive adult? Here are two truisms: overcoming obstacles brings strength; and few adults, let alone children, can get by with no one at all.

At that time these thoughts were the basis of my intention and I had no real notion of the fundamental importance of solid values to the process of learning itself. But with experience it has become more and more clear that the efforts being made on behalf of the positive, inner self are of enormous benefit to all the manifestations of the whole, visible person, including the understanding of academic subjects. The observation of wishes, actions, consequences and the complex interplay of people and things upon one another are at the base of comprehending our own part in the total picture. The clarity available from the simple practice of drawing back from events to look calmly at the picture and see where it can be changed is at the base of leading a balanced and purposeful life, and this practice, or discipline, is of great worth when applied to academic effort. Moreover, the calm, which is created by the habit of reflection, brings to the learner a capacity for observation unfettered by the habits of worry or mind flitting. In this way, a strong capacity for detached concentration is developed.

Respect for children

I would probably not have expressed these thoughts quite in this form when I started teaching. In the early 1970s the concept of holism was scarcely even named. Things were still compartmentalised. At school we learned history and geography, French and maths, subject separation prevailed in the curriculum, so that in terms of values what came into the classroom was not the large moral questions but a simple set of school rules which, incidentally, did not apply to adults. Children were required, for example, to show respect while very often not being given it. Quite young children can see they are being deceived if they are told to show what they do not remotely feel. They understand perfectly that if it means they must hold a door open for someone they fear as a bully rather than respect as a human being, their outward demeanour must belie their inner perception. The same applies to the practice, still widespread, of teachers arriving late for school assembly and talking during it. Children, of course, are not allowed to do these things and they see that the world is a place where the odds are stacked against them. Such behaviour is comparable with military discipline: 'Do as I say, not as I do, and take that look off your face!' and it is the seedbed for cynicism. Thus, alongside a wish to help with the process of observation and inward looking I saw an obligation upon adults to participate equally. I also saw that rules must apply to all and be seen to be applied fairly for children to realise that their own struggles and efforts are supported and shared by the adults around them.

I see the place of values in developing the whole person, both the rational aspects and the inner self. This is not yet the moment to go into which values I am talking about. Most teachers would applaud the notion of positive values and many would still mean by that some variation on, 'Best foot forward, for the good of the school!' or perhaps, 'Play up and play the game!' – which is not at all what I mean. We shall come to a clearer definition of what I mean later; meanwhile, the importance of shared values cannot be too strongly emphasised. I see values as the foundation of education, of the healthy development of children, indeed of the strength of the national community, and I see the absence of a harmonious and unified set of positive values as the beginning of chaos and distress. This is a time of great moral confusion in which organised religions are losing their influence and no clear ethical arbiter has emerged to replace them, beyond the arbitrary and commercial one of television and film. Fortunately, positive values are shared by all ethical persuasions, and can be understood and applied by everyone within the small community of the school and the large one of the nation.

It seemed to me that the great omission in most educational theory was the condition and vision of the child. All the focus was on programming. Consideration of the character, emotions and outlook, of the ability to make choices, the ability to acquire the information in order to make the choices, was absent. You could say the heart was not being attended to, all was external, and the focus on educating the head alone left out heart and hands to the detriment of the whole human being. My concern was also to counterbalance the prevailing idea of happiness only from material success, and all the concentration on the external, with the capacity of each child to discover or perhaps rediscover their inherent harmony and comprehension My phrase for this is *the child as reflective learner*.

My assumption is that the most enjoyable behaviour is that which brings about the greatest happiness for the greatest number and enables children to be at ease in the wider community as well as in the context of the family and school. My concurrent assumption is that children are inherently positive and valuable although they may sometimes do inappropriate or discordant things. It seems to me that the ability to observe how one's behaviour affects oneself and others, and to modify it if necessary so that the realisation of one's own wishes is harmonious with living in the world, is perhaps the greatest feat of balance required of us – and the most essential.

The condition and vision of the children is of course affected by everything around them; they are constantly bombarded with powerful and seductive messages. The values education policy note for the staff at West Kidlington School says:

'Children are repeatedly given the impression that happiness is obtainable only from a material world. They are encouraged to experience life in an external world full of noise and activity. Impressions of a violent and selfish society leave their mark as the child develops into adolescence. Symptoms of pupils' stress are seen as children find it difficult to listen attentively ... Social relationships suffer as the child often fails to appreciate that building relationships is their own responsibility.

'As a school community we believe the ethos of the school should be built on core values such as *honesty, respect, happiness, responsibility, tolerance,* and *peace*.... They are the basis for the social, intellectual, emotional, spiritual and moral development of the whole child. [Longer term] they can grow to be stable, educated and civil adults.'

A curious response, though perhaps not entirely unexpected, has been for people to ask, 'but doesn't it all take up *school time*?' as though the effort towards harmony is not perceived as worthwhile in its own right. Happily I can justify it in terms of the improvement in the children's concentration, in their ability to work through problems, and in the calmness with which they approach their schoolwork. In addition, the school inspectors from Ofsted [the government regulatory body] observed that the fine quality of the children's academic and artistic schoolwork was a direct result of the values effort. Calm, happy, focused children produce good work. They produce it because they enjoy it. The film that Central Television news made about the school showed children saying, 'we're happy, we enjoy our school-work'. And if happiness from harmonious surroundings and honest endeavour were not an end in itself, our high place in the league tables satisfies the questioner.

Positive values at West Kidlington School

I came to West Kidlington School in 1992 from the post of chief inspector of the schools advisory service on the Isle of Wight. Many found this decision incomprehensible since the status of inspector is much greater than that of schoolmaster and the usual career path would regard such a move as backwards. However, I had spent enough time looking at schools and their difficulties and was becoming more and more clear about how I saw the future, which is what we shall be talking about in this book. It was time for me to get back to the practical, hands-on world of the classroom and see how much of my vision could reach practical realisation.

Kidlington is a village that has become more or less a dormitory suburb for the city of Oxford. It was built mostly in the 1930s and is not especially wealthy, indeed the school population includes many from single parent homes and the children often need special help with early learning skills such as reading, as well as with their emotional distresses. Kidlington is famous because the millionaire businessman Sir Richard Branson has a home there and because it has an airport for private light aircraft which claims to have more take-offs and landings per square metre of airstrip per day than any other airport in the world except London Heathrow (although none of this has any noticeable impact on the 480 children of West Kidlington Primary school). In common with most of the people of the area I find my way into Sir Richard's garden for the parties he generously gives in the summer for locals, and my attempt to thrust a petition for funds into his hands is skilfully foiled.

When I arrived at the school there was an expectation that I would generate new ideas. We needed a shared vision about creating a school of excellence. Aspects of the curriculum needed to be co-ordinated and the staff were working somewhat independently, so the immediate task was to define their roles and get them to work together. Curriculum managers had to be trained. The school needed re-energising. Two years before I arrived it had suffered a dramatic change in the form of a fire and some classes were still being held in temporary buildings. Perhaps the fact that we had to have so much rebuilding offered some sort of metaphor for the restructuring that we did elsewhere. Another visual change came when the parents voted to return to having a school uniform. It is blue and red, bright and functional, and it helps to weld the community together as well as ensuring that children who are not well off do not stand out.

I set about explaining to my new staff what I have written here: that the positive values emphasis was to be pivotal, that we would all participate, that the parents would be involved too, and that I looked forward to an era of harmony and co-operation. Fortunately they were with me. I have been extremely lucky throughout my time at West Kidlington school with the support I have received from staff, governors and parents, and in an era when school governors have increasing influence I would like to acknowledge the importance of their positive input and helpfulness. Since its rebuilding, the school is light and airy, the foyer and the hall have glass roofs, and it is a most heartening place to work. The entrance is welcoming, the main school is bright and pleasing, in fact it gained a great deal from the catastrophe of the fire in which luckily no one was hurt since it happened at a weekend. Our many local and international visitors comment on the calm atmosphere and the school's attractiveness and we are always happy to welcome them.

New appointments during my tenure have been similarly harmonious and I hope that everyone who has worked in the school during this time has learned positively from it. I have always recommended people for appointment as much for the qualities they bring as for their paper qualifications. Sometimes if I had followed their CV I might have said, 'no, there are people more qualified, more experienced,' but I have selected when I have been impressed with a person, as a person, and when I've felt that they have qualities that the children would benefit from enormously. Teachers who have worked particularly well within the spirit and intention are many and only a few have space to record their views here. To all of them, however, I would like to offer my warm thanks for being part of it.

A post script

In 1998 I was asked by my local education authority to help support a school south of Oxford in Blackbird Leys. The school had been through a series of crises and desperately needed strong yet sensitive leadership. Schools in challenging areas of social priority need stability in all senses of the word. I worked with the dedicated staff to introduce a values approach. They gave me their confidence and allowed me to steer them through a difficult period of internal adjustment – the head teacher had just retired on health grounds – and to continue to face the unremitting demands of the school's catchment area.

A calm, purposeful, reflective school environment was established, which nurtured staff and pupils. Tensions subsided, teachers began to enjoy their teaching again and pupils were able to feel more secure in classes that carefully established a negotiated code of conduct built on respect. Emphasis was given to the positive aspects of the children. It is equally important for children and adults to discover their inner qualities; it raises everyone's self-esteem, everyone's self-worth. Once adults and children are in touch with their essence, they can celebrate differences and enjoy them, instead of trying to do away with them.

The positive ethos, which I believe allows everything to happen, soon wrought its magic again and the school is now running in a different way. The change arrived quite quickly, showing that it was in reality what everyone wanted. The children stopped fighting, the staff started to be calm, harmony was restored – and there was another Quiet Revolution.

There have been other and even more diverse situations in which the principles for a Quiet Revolution have been of great use. In my work as a consultant for UNICEF I have been invited to speak in places as diverse as Mauritius, India and the USA. My visit to Mauritius was especially delightful: here was a nation beginning a new phase in its history, building itself up, starting many new enterprises that required a more formal approach to education. The people were concerned not to import Western materialism along with the aspects of Western life they were courting. The question was how to promote the idea of a technical education system, with its new and heavy demands, without seeing the only goal as jobs and money?

The constant investigation and evaluation of positive concepts, the habit and practice of silent reflection, and the special school assemblies, which together make up the values programme, were eagerly embraced by the teachers and government officials I talked to in the wonderful week I spent there. As in West Kidlington and Blackbird Leys, so in Mauritius. The same story applies in different degrees and in different detail wherever I have spoken. I have found people eager to build more strongly, to support young people and children, and indeed to join with them in making the personal effort.

From what I have seen abroad I believe this model to be transferable to any school in the world and any age group. In this book we shall be talking about a principle in detail and in particular, which however has very general application. We shall also be talking about the possibility of a Quiet Revolution taking place at home. Wherever there is consensus on the aspiration for a high ideal for creating harmony, variety and balance within a community, for celebrating difference and yet pulling together for the good of the whole – there is fertile ground for the ideas that work so well at West Kidlington School.

A note on management

People sometimes ask me how I get the teaching and other staff to join me in doing things in a new way, to take on the challenging task of rethinking and regenerating a school's values. The first thing, of course, is my own commitment and my own caring. I have to be, and be seen to be, someone who is aspiring to high effort. When people can recognise that, they can commit themselves. Luckily I have found that in general people are incredibly supportive.

I am always available to listen, available and also human, authentic and caring. It's important to be open at an emotional and social level. However it's risky, people can take liberties; they can sometimes take advantage. This is where a certain distance comes in. It is a difficult balance, but when you get it right you are ensuring good working relationships. Despite the openness and egalitarianism, the school situation is far from *laissez-faire*, there are very high implicit expectations. People soon know if something is not right. You have to negotiate how an organisation is, and then maintain it.

The main thing about being a good leader is the ability to look forward, know what is going on, and guide others in that way. You have to delegate logistically and psychologically, then everyone has a stake. Ask for updates on what people are doing; ask about their new curriculum plans. Show the people working with you that they're important. When you devolve certain responsibilities or tasks, never give people the feeling that having done so you're no longer interested – people soon get discouraged if you do that. Acknowledge when something's working well, for example in assembly. Write little notes. But it's also an important aspect of leadership that if you delegate, you must still take the blame if something goes wrong. You must shield and support your staff, the moment you stop you're in deep water because then they don't trust you.

I haven't created a dependency culture, actually the main thing is just being there to give the much-needed smile. Teachers generally are feeling got at and the head teacher must counter that constantly by giving the opposite impression. I simply provide the framework in which everyone operates. I offer genuine good wishes, I acknowledge hard work and effort, and I take people seriously. You have to be able to offer a lightness at times, you have to show your own humanity – and you have to be prepared to say sorry. In short, my idea of being a leader and a manager has to do with appreciating all people, regardless of their supposed status.

... and a note on the use of the word spirituality

Words that become fashionable often have their meanings eroded by excessive or careless use and at the moment it seems as though the word spirituality could be heading towards this fate. Spirituality is, of course, difficult to define, and in any case who are we, simple primary school teachers, to claim to teach such an elusive, imponderable thing? But despite these difficulties I would like to offer some thoughts on what we are aspiring towards under this heading.

Spirituality, defined as the aspiration/wish for transcendence, is within all of us and can be sought in houses of religion and many other places. People look for it in art, pictures or music, or in a distorted way in the material world of sex or drugs. It comes from the basic longing to be transported, or elevated. But though the need is inherent and must find nourishment, spirituality also needs to be worked on. Though it is natural, the perceptive capacity for it has to be built up.

That is why the children at West Kidlington practise observation, reflective stillness, and the habit of considering carefully all sides of a question. They practise emptying their minds and then focusing upon one positive concept. The progression in the morning assemblies was described in another context by the visionary Sir George Trevelyan, 'stillness – tranquillity – peace – a trinity of kindred states, which include body, heart and mind'. The mastery of this enables the children to contact the still centre within them and gives them the option of gaining access to it for greater comprehension or in times of emotional trouble. It enables the children to use their inherent ability in their own way.

The Kidlington Blueprint in its totality provides children with the mechanisms, means and vocabulary for what is often referred to as *emotional intelligence* – the ability to consider one's own emotional condition and affect it. They can talk about their feelings and they can even talk about them almost dispassionately. They can look at incidents and events and their part in them, and see how their part affected the whole. It is invaluable.

If children did finger exercises to make their hands supple, some might become fine pianists, others might become fine wood carvers or whatever they wished – they would have the means to use their hands to create what they wanted. They could use their hands more subtly and infinitely more variously than if they had not made them capable. Throughout the exercising of the fingers the next step would also have been made clear to them: the suppleness thus gained was to be used for the creation of something unequivocally beautiful.

In the same way, we believe that the constant positive exercising of the mind and perception refines the children's own ability to use their inherent creativity, or *spirituality*, in their own ways.

Comments from teachers

The rest of this chapter offers reflections from others on the particular approach at West Kidlington.

Linda and John Heppenstall

The first two comments come from among the longest serving members of staff and represent something of a phenomenon: a couple who teach happily together every day. John Heppenstall has been at the school for 20 years, and his wife Linda for around 15 years. She was a supply teacher while their daughter was small and then she joined the staff full-time. Thus they have continuity of experience and can talk about how the school has evolved in recent years.

Linda Heppenstall This was always a nice school and the changes that have happened have been very gradual. To begin with Neil would say, 'Let's have a moment of quiet,' that's how I remember the start of the reflection thing. It was very much an evolution. I remember when he first came that I thought he was a manager and not a teacher.

John Heppenstall Neil has changed. He used to have a briefcase and a Filofax.

Linda When the new building opened, that was when things started to move.

John The first part of the process was to produce a mission statement, what we thought the school was about, what education meant for children. It became clear that we were to underpin the whole thing with values. Neil formalised it within the curriculum. Of course, in most decent schools the teaching of values is implicit, but here, since the changes, values teaching is a core subject.

Linda The school has become much more integrated. The mission statement proposed a whole-school approach. Before that, the staff all lived in their own little rooms and if you were teaching values you'd do your own thing. No one helped the staff. The children on the playground showed much more aggression; the difference this has made to playground behaviour is the most immediately obvious one, although there are others.

John The year groups [teachers of children of the same age] got together to enable setting [grouping by ability] and to ensure there was equality of provision across year groups. There were weekly planning meetings.

Linda We started to work together as people.

John We never used to have staff meetings and suddenly we were pulling together.

Linda We went along with it because we got a feeling it was good.

John We were all made to feel part of a team.

Linda We all got new responsibility, I got Personal and Social Education, I love it, it was just me! When the new subject responsibilities were given out, it seemed as though everyone had got what they wanted.

John Next September we've all got new classes. It fits together like a jigsaw. I can say I've never experienced such high morale. I'm sure the children must feel it as well, they must feel more positive.

Linda Before this, no one mentioned values. The interesting thing is that we decided as a staff that we would look at the needs of children and when we did, we found they were the needs of the staff as well. My understanding of relationships and myself is very different nowadays.

John Previously only the head and the deputy head took assemblies, but now we all do – and we all teach spirituality. It's in the mainstream. Actually the staff were never fazed or threatened by it; if the consent hadn't been there it wouldn't have happened. The whole atmosphere of the staff, co-operation and working together and saying *yes*, carries you through. You set up your day at assemblies. Suddenly, when the National Curriculum came in you had to do RE – and people liked this way of doing it. It pre-empts bad behaviour.

Linda You've got a way of talking to children if they misbehave that gives them a reason to behave well. It's all about relationships. They're learning about their feelings, their range of emotions, what they have in common with each other, how they differ – so that really, they're learning to understand themselves better and get to know who they are.

Betty Brands

Betty Brands is a humorous, down-to-earth young Scotswoman. Among her most demanding tasks at West Kidlington was handling the death from leukaemia of one of her ten-year-old pupils. The little girl had continued to attend morning school until she became too ill; her classmates knew about her condition, some of them visited her at home and they all sent cards. When she died, the news was given to all the children in the school by their class teachers in their individual year groups. Betty Brands had to tell the girl's classmates. She, the school office manager and head teacher and I had all visited the child at home. Many school staff attended the girl's funeral and during the remaining weeks of the term Mrs Brands often talked to the children about her. She continued to be part of the normal school day, 'Oh, Louise would have liked that, wouldn't she!' or 'Louise would have laughed at that, that's just her sort of joke!'

A table was arranged in the classroom as a sort of shrine, with Louise's drawings and writings displayed around a photograph of her. Within three or four days of the child's passing, most of her classmates could talk about her without crying.

'Miss, you know what, when Louise and I ——— !' or 'Do you know what Louise said?' 'After a week,' says Betty Brands, 'the children were still a bit weepy about her, but by then it was for the good times. We had pictures of her and we still said, 'Good afternoon Louise', when we took the register, right up until the end of that term.'

Here, Mrs Brands speaks on the subject of discipline.

Betty Brands Before I came here I thought discipline was something head teachers did, but here we all do it and nobody raises their voice. If a child hasn't done the desired action or behaviour you just have to speak to them and that by itself will upset them so much they don't do it again. It takes a lot of work and a lot of trust from the child. There's no need to raise your voice. I must say it's bizarre! I've never seen it before, a place where there's no need to raise your voice. I've seen both ways – I've seen the inner city sort, screaming and shouting down a corridor, and I've also seen this. It's so lovely to come into a school and just walk, and the children are walking. It's lovely not seeing the bullying. They're all little individuals, and that's the most powerful thing, they're being who they are, to the best they can.

Comments from visitors

West Kidlington Primary School often has visitors who come to look at how it works. They may be from abroad or from different parts of Great Britain; they may be educationalists or teachers, or they may be from religious or spiritual organisations.

Visitors from north London

The group talking here include almost all the categories mentioned above. There are two women and one man and their observations have a common quality: wonder. They all found the atmosphere remarkable. One of the women had moved from being a head teacher to take up the administrative role of adviser and said the visit had made her homesick to run a school again. For various reasons their identities cannot be disclosed.

First visitor The quietness is impressive. It's not usual to see a primary school with no noise, but with the silence not being enforced. The children are working quietly but there's no feeling of being kept down, they're very confident – and yet they're very polite.

I asked a child which of her teachers she liked best and she said, 'I like all the teachers.' I found that marvellous! In other schools children will always say, 'I hate so-and-so.' They've always got someone they don't get on with, but here it really doesn't seem like that. Another very unusual thing is that when you talk to the children they don't immediately answer, they think first. Such confidence! The answer they give you has been considered. The children are a lot more relaxed, so they're more receptive. They feel valued because of the way they're treated, so their self-esteem is great.

Second visitor I'm totally overwhelmed! I felt something very special here.

First visitor It's right to put the values first. It seems so obvious. Education is so concerned with targets that we're losing sight of the children as people: at the moment they're just numbers. Do we really want a nation [of children] who can write a story in 45 minutes, and do we really think that's all that matters? It's like having to produce so many cars an hour. The values deal with what's inside. Literacy and numeracy are the next layer; they're not the first. We've ignored what's inside for a long time.

Sometimes children can be a bit fazed when they don't know you but here they're all quite open and honest about how they felt they were doing. The most amazing thing for me this morning was a boy asking me for help with his maths, and I'm a complete stranger. He said, 'I'm a bit stuck', and asked me if I would look at it for him. They obviously have a lot of visitors; our presence in the classrooms didn't disrupt anything they were doing. The children are very genuine with everybody. I was just a passing adult and he needed help with his maths. If they can ask absolutely anyone for help like that, think how much that will help them throughout their lives.

Third visitor What is obvious in this school is that they care about the children. It might sound strange to say that but it isn't always the case everywhere. It's also very refreshing to see a school saying 'we know what's best', because so many don't have the confidence to say that any more. Here, there's a very clear definition of the ethos. The official line, the establishment line, is that high standards are measurable, they're all to do with attainment, but here high standards mean a lot more than that. Mind you, it's hard work! It throws up some tricky questions for adults as well as children. I can see you would have to engage with it fully if you wanted to take part in it at all.

An academic researcher from the USA

The special qualities of the school have been the subject of several theses, including Mr Hawkes'. It is visited by teachers, teacher trainers, people from religious institutions and overseas students. This American academic is concerned with perceptions of leading and managing. He especially notices the consensus among the staff and the continuity of approach. He has been visiting West Kidlington and other British schools for more than six years.

US Researcher A clear sense of purpose is apparent even from a very short visit. There are so many reminders of it. I walked in this morning to see the word *care* in the hall, and it's everywhere – you go into the classrooms and you see common themes expressed. Not every school has a common commitment to a mutual goal; the great thing here is cohesiveness. In this environment there's no sense of upset, of people with different agendas headed in different directions. The interesting thing is that it isn't imposed from above, there wouldn't be unanimity of purpose if it were. The structure has encouraged discussion and co-operation.

Every school has unique characteristics and here there is this purpose and calm everywhere. I think it is important to note also that the school has developed with the parents; they are very much part of it. Both in the United States and in Great Britain schools are trying to stay ahead of a wave of educational reform. Education is not static. What is going on here, however, provides great security through continuity. This almost certainly benefits the adults as much as the children.

PC Jayne Newman, West Kidlington Constabulary

A community policewoman, PC Newman runs sessions to teach children to trust the police and to tell a policeman or a dependable adult if they need help.

Police Constable Newman At West Kidlington they're very friendly, the staff are positive and when you go in you are always welcomed. I feel part of it when I go there, I'm not made to feel I'm in the way. The children themselves are very calm. They don't get over-excited and they pay good attention.

Sheila Kitchen, veteran school worker

Thirty years as a dinner lady have given Mrs Kitchen insights into school life. The current staff of two women for a few hours at lunchtime used to be nine for the whole morning. These days she is semi-retired, and helps the teacher on dinner duty to ensure that the children eat their dinners.

Sheila Kitchen At the beginning we cooked everything on the premises and your hands were always sore from peeling swedes, cutting up cabbages, chopping things up. It all took hours! It's all different now, and not nearly so many kitchen staff.

I still enjoy being with the children very much. Most of the time they're very good. The little ones I like, the six-year-olds especially. They always come and tell me when it's their birthday or what's happening in their lives, and they like to hold my hand. I love watching them play. Not very often, just sometimes, there's a fight. You'll see two of the boys on the floor and you go up to them and say, 'what's the problem?' They'll say, 'he's got my football' or 'he's called me a name.' I get them to apologise to each other and shake hands.

The children often tell me their troubles. Sometimes it's their love life; somebody's dumped them and they're heartbroken. You'd think it was the end of the world, it's the same when friends fall out.

I don't come across any cheeky children; really there's a lot of respect. I say to the children, 'If you want respect from me you've got to give me respect,' and they do. You shouldn't talk down *to* children, you should talk to them. The words they're learning [positive value words] will hopefully help them on their way.

I say to the leavers, you've got a good grounding at West Kidlington and I hope you'll take it with you. They're all good really. When I worked in the kitchen, they were so well-mannered.

Alex Vincent, school caretaker

Alex Vincent has worked at West Kidlington Primary school for ten years. He fixes everything that needs fixing, brings in and supervises other practical people such as plumbers and builders. He also does rural watercolours, which are displayed around the school and admired by many visitors. His small workshop is tucked away behind the Junior cloakroom and crammed with tools, cleaning materials, and seedlings for the school. On a shelf among the tools Alex has a hand-made greetings card from six-year-old Georgina thanking him for keeping the school so neat. It has a picture of a sweeping brush on the front and one of a lavatory cistern inside. 'I get two or three like this a month,' says Alex proudly. He likes the children, and from conversational exchanges between them it is clear they like him too.

Alex Vincent The kids are smashing. When I walk round the village they greet me in the street, even the ones who've left. It makes you feel part of the community. It's as though the school goes on outside as well!

THE KIDLINGTON BLUEPRINT

At the end of each chapter are some notes for parents. Unlike the others, this particular one is not a summary of the West Kidlington experience set out as a possible blueprint for use at home. Instead, it's a summary of what the school is about.

- The child as reflective learner.

- The practice of contemplation, reflection and consideration before taking action.

- Adults as partners in and supporters of children's growing-up and development.

- The building of mind, body, heart and soul.

- The work of the adult world: to enable the next generation to grow positively, strongly and joyfully.

- Emotional stability at school and in the home.

- Sensitive listening.

- Calm discussion.

- Spiritual endeavour.

These are some of the major topics of this book, set within a picture of a profoundly happy place of learning.

Chapter 2

A Day in the Life

8.05am: Monday

IT IS A SUNNY DAY IN MARCH AND ALREADY THE WEST KIDLINGTON PRIMARY School car park is almost full of teachers' cars. Head teacher Neil Hawkes arrives as the eight o'clock news is ending on his car radio and takes the penultimate parking space. Some of the staff are already inside working in their classrooms, some are hurrying into the driveway carrying boxes of papers and schoolbooks, some are arriving by bike. At 8.15am Mrs Lobban, the office manager, arrives. She has driven the fourteen miles from the village near Thame where she lives; she says good morning and moves briskly on: in her own eyes she's late. Pretty much everyone starts work on arrival and the first mechanical sound is that of the photocopier. Betty Brands has a stack of material to copy and as usual the machine has to be refilled with paper: the cost of photocopy paper is one of Neil Hawkes' recurrent headaches.

The foyer has a very particular atmosphere at this time of day: it's a theatre before the audience comes in, it's a shop about to open. The impression of anticipation may be intensified because it is also the beginning of the last week of the spring term and the Easter holidays are in prospect. Teaching and non-teaching staff are coming into school and moving straight through the foyer and the place is bright and energetic – though strangely, it is almost silent. When people see each other they say, 'Morning, nice weekend?' 'Yes thanks!', two or three words more, then they hurry on.

8.25am: children arriving

From about 8.25am the children start arriving, a surprising number of them on foot in unaccompanied groups of two or three. Most of them are talking animatedly about their friends and their friends' doings in a lively way.

Many bring in the weekend's crop of supermarket tokens and crisp packets that have been saved up to put into collection boxes towards the purchase of essential schoolbooks or computers. Slightly later come streams of parents with the children who are being brought to school along with their younger siblings who haven't started there yet. The pupils are easily identified by their navy and red uniforms and their purposeful demeanour. It is rare for anyone to be late. Most of the children arrive at school in good order and ready for the day and the parents say they never have any trouble getting them there.

A mother and a boy of about seven scan the week's menus posted outside the front entrance and decide which of the dinners he will take at school this week. Alex the caretaker is also at the front entrance and in his customary mood: philosophical combined with grumpy. He is putting black rubbish bags into a huge wheely bin and remarks that some of the children from Year Six usually help him with it, 'but as soon as the nice weather comes they've got better things to do.' (Amazingly, these same children have also appointed themselves rubbish pickers-up and voluntarily clear up the playground every day. As a result it is always immaculate.)

Headteacher Neil Hawkes stands in the foyer to greet the arriving parents and children and hear the news that comes in with the morning. Parents often use this time of day to speak of their anxieties, even to the extent of confiding their family breakdowns. Marriage and relationship difficulties have a terrible effect on the emotions of children and hence on their academic ability, and the borders between psychology, social work and teaching have probably never been less clear than they are now. Teachers usually know about such situations in advance of the adult explanation for even if the children involved have not spoken of it directly their distraction will have told its own tale. In such circumstances children are visibly upset even in such a supportive environment as this one and their concentration inevitably suffers too.

A mother has come to tell Mr Hawkes that her husband had a car accident at the weekend and is in intensive care in hospital in Southampton, 70 miles away. She is crying and they go into his office to speak privately. Neil Hawkes says he gets to school earlier on Mondays because parents often have things to tell him that have happened at the weekend. 'Monday is especially dramatic,' he says, 'I'm not quite sure why. It's as though the community has to bring its dramas back to school.'

Since he always conducts the Monday assembly and must get the hall ready and set up the music (today from *Titanic*), the extra early start is essential if he is also to be available to listen to people's troubles. Some good things are brought to him too: two of the Year Six boys won swimming awards at the weekend and want to show the shields they got. One of them is dyspraxic (an impairment in the control of the motor system) yet swims for two hours every morning, a special triumph. Out in the foyer three more boys have formed a ragged sort of queue to get their weekend crop of crisp packets for schoolbooks into the collection box. 'I've got *lots!*' says a six-year-old, proudly stuffing them through the cardboard letterbox ahead of his friend.

West Kidlington Primary School is about six miles from the ancient university city of Oxford in a small satellite town. West Kidlington itself is somewhat unprepossessing and is stuck on to the side of a much older village, which has one or two splendid houses. It has no obvious centre but an uninspiring row of shops in a pedestrian zone, a car showroom, a garage, and on Fridays and Saturdays a small street market, which is strong on plants and birthday cards.

The school is in the middle of a housing estate and has pleasant grounds with a playing field, a playground, and a small, enclosed garden where a rose bed has been created as a memorial to Louise, a West Kidlington pupil who died of leukaemia at the age of ten. The rose bed contains a commemorative stone carved for her by one of the fathers. Bordering the playing field there is high wire netting to prevent balls flying into the gardens of the local householders, though sometimes the balls go wide even of the netting and have to be retrieved. The highest visible structures are a broadcasting mast and a short, modern church tower. Playing field, playground and school are often flown over by light aircraft because of the nearby Kidlington airport, which is used only by private planes.

The main school was substantially rebuilt in 1990 after a fire, which damaged buildings, and the buildings are now mostly of wood and glass, somewhat Scandinavian looking, and maintained adequately rather than luxuriously. Most of them could do with a lick of paint and Alex Vincent says the older buildings that survived the fire were meant to be temporary about 30 years ago and now cause problems because their roofs let in water.

The main school buildings are grouped around a small courtyard with the school garden and the school pond at its centre. Garden and pond are maintained by Alex, who takes cuttings and grows some plants from seed in his hideout near the Year Two cloakroom. New buildings were put up after the fire but were soon found to be inadequate. Of the independent, auxiliary classrooms around the school playground some are wooden, some are prefabricated terrapins, all could do with a lick of paint. More buildings become necessary as the number of children increases, new activities are introduced (extra music, for example) and the special needs teaching requires more space.

The foyer in the new building has a glass roof that can be opened in hot weather and the main entrance is so pretty that visitors are amazed to find that West Kidlington is a state-funded school. Any account of the hallway must include the fabulously arty glass clock over the staffroom door. It is large and beautiful, its face painted with the moon and sun and lesser planets, light pours through it from skylights within the staff room. At night, from an electric source underneath it, it provides an exuberant welcome even on the greyest day. However, it's often wrong. A local watchmaker mends it for them but they have to wait until he has a bit of spare time.

9am: the school day begins

A big collage about the Oxford Playhouse *Cinderella* pantomime receives a favourable review from Neil Hawkes' visitors for today: a group of north London educationalists who have come to look at the values programme in action. 'The children's work is everywhere, always nicely presented, very lively,' says one. On the wall there are also photographs of children in assembly; on low tables there are photograph albums recording school trips and events, silver cups, shields for winning six-a-side tag netball; information about the school guide dog; and copies of the new prospectus. There is always some charity collecting box or other, a petition to sign, and the boxes for the supermarket tokens. The foyer is a place of businesslike activity. It is the first place for parents, visiting teachers, delivery people, technicians who have come to install or fix computers, people who have come to set up a new lighting system.

The administrators are the focus of the foyer and their office has a window, which you must pass to get to the rest of the school. Mrs Lobban says, 'You really see the school from here'. She is blonde, motherly and smiling, and she talks to the children kindly, 'All right there my lovely?' and firmly, 'Of course I will, but what's the word that's been missed out?' (Most likely *please*.) She defines the office function simply. 'We're the first in the firing line.' Mrs Byford, the dark, slim finance manager, is concerned less with the school population passing the main office window and more with accountancy in her own, adjacent office. The administrators love the school and their work, which they will tell you is amazingly varied (as if to prove this point, two of the dinner ladies appear with a bouquet of flowers for a teacher who is going on maternity leave). It involves a great deal of pastoral care of the school population alongside the standard office tasks. They also enjoy handing over to the children at lunchtime, of which more later.

Every practical and dramatic question comes first to the office window. Tradesmen may need to be redirected to Alex Vincent's room; dignitaries arrive to see Mr Hawkes; there are deliveries to accept or redirect; people coming for job interviews; parents wanting to talk to one or other of the teachers or to the head teacher himself; sick children who want a parent or carer to come and take them home. These last are usually brought by a well child at the request of a teacher. 'Excuse me Mrs Lobban, this is Luke, he's got a sore throat, Mrs Brown said please will you phone home for him.' 'Of course I will, thank you for bringing him, you go back to your class now and tell Mrs Brown he's being looked after.' And to Luke with the sore throat, 'How are you, poor thing! Don't worry, I'll phone your mum straight away and we'll get you home.'

But the phoning may go on for some time. The sick child waits crumpled in a chair, often quite upset, but the administrators can't always get through to a parent or carer immediately. For some children they have six phone numbers for adult contacts; for others (like Luke) they only have one. They try again and again, and periodically they make sure the child is still all right, explain what's going on, make soothing noises, offer drinks. Luke's mum was not at home and it was nearly an hour and at least three attempts to get through before Luke recalled that it was her day at Further Education college. There is simply no hope of tracking down a student in the labyrinth of a college and messages are unlikely to reach their destination. The administrators said none of this to Luke but made a note that when they next contacted his mother they must ask for more phone numbers for their list. At this point with a very ill child there could have been a more serious difficulty, but, just as they were beginning to feel concerned, Luke's mum phoned in anyway, and they got her to come and fetch him. From start to finish it had taken nearly two hours, which is not unusual.

10.20am: Infants break time

Morning break times vary for Infants and Juniors and naturally the weather determines what they can do. Today it is sunny and the big playground is full of children playing energetically, laughing, skipping, giving piggy-backs, playing tig, playing counting games in pairs, running back and forth. Some of the games are wholly incomprehensible. A little girl is leading another little girl around the playground on a piece of rope; both of them are smiling happily. A six-year-old boy in a fireman's helmet charges about on his own. Behind a low wall five boys are hiding, two of them with the fashionably loose shoelaces. They are as excited as plotters and one of them says cryptically, 'she's not *dead*.' In a corner of the playground a small group of children is engaged in an elaborate ritual of scissor-jumping to a rhyme.

> 'Cat's got the measles
> Dog's got the flu
> Chicken pox
> Chicken pox
> So have you!'

If their feet are apart when the rhyme ends they forfeit an item of clothing, which they must throw into the middle of the ring. Some of the boys have lost pullover and tie and are down to one sock, and the teacher on playground duty is keeping an eye on it. Soon the group, which started with six children, has attracted nine more, but fortunately the morning break is edging towards the end of its ten minutes so there is little time left. Before long the bell rings for school to resume and the children start to go back indoors, an orderly departure. For his part, however, Alex Vincent believes they wait for the hand bell to be rung for lessons before all rushing to the toilets at once and flooding them.

The children treat Alex Vincent with respect but they are not afraid to approach him and report problems; this is an aspect of the skill of dealing with adults that they are learning more or less constantly. They demonstrate it by making their request politely, in the expectation of having it met.

Boys Mr Vincent, excuse me, all the boys' toilets are blocked in the cloakroom!

Alex Vincent What, every one? Again?

Boys Yes.

Alex Vincent Why don't you use the ones in the main school, then?

Boys They're blocked in the cloakroom!

Alex Vincent What's wrong, somebody put too much paper down?

Boys There's lots of toilet paper and there's water high up and they won't flush.

Alex Vincent I'll fix them at the end of the afternoon when you've all gone home. Use the ones in the main school, they're working all right. And don't use so much paper! There's no need to use a whole roll when you go.'

Boys We don't.

The boys seem disconsolate, but set off towards the main school. 'I look after them like a Dutch Uncle,' says Alex Vincent. 'The teachers too. The teachers are just the same, they come to me for everything: their car's got a puncture, the roof's leaking … Mind you, if you're moaning they won't come near you, that's why I complain a lot.' On this showing, however, Alex's strategy is not entirely successful.

10.40am: Juniors break time

The games are more sophisticated than at Infants break time and some of the children simply walk decorously around arm in arm. Three of the youngest girls set off for the office to ask for jobs, but Mrs Lobban has nothing to give them. 'Anything you'd like us to take to the teachers?' they ask. 'Not this time, my lovelies, maybe I'll have something for you tomorrow,' she says, and they return to the playground. 'They're very trustworthy, those three,' remarks Sue Lobban. 'They did the raffle at Christmas, absolutely perfectly. All the accounts and everything, meticulously kept.' At 10.50am the office suddenly gets very busy; teachers are in and carrying notes and messages. A father comes into the foyer and stops at the window to ask if he can put his daughter down on the list for a nursery place, but the nursery places have all gone. There are 26 children in the morning session of the West Kidlington nursery and 26 in the afternoon session, and a substantial waiting list. Mrs Lobban explains Oxfordshire County Council's admissions policy to him, and that the names for admission to the nursery are drawn out of a hat.

'Last time,' she says by way of consolation, 'we got four or five extra places from people whose children were in a private nursery and who decided to keep them there after all. It could happen again, don't give up.' But the father can be neither consoled nor convinced, and keeps asking the same questions. 'We'll let you know if any of the places aren't taken up,' is all Mrs Lobban can offer. At last he goes. A mother turns up with a broken dolphin badge [the school emblem] hoping there might be a replacement for her young daughter. 'Only she liked it very much,' she explains, apologetically. 'I might be able to find you another,' says Mrs Lobban. 'Just leave it with me, will you?'

11.30am: morning lessons

For an adult, crossing the school playground to one of the outside class-rooms is a pleasant journey, not least because it is customary for the door to the destination classroom to start opening before it is reached. This demonstrates the practical truth of the visiting north London teacher's remark, 'Every adult who comes in is considered valuable by the children.' What happens when the adult reaches the open door is that the waiting child will say, 'Can I help?' not in the officious manner of shop assistants, but genuinely. 'Who are you looking for?' they ask politely. 'Oh, yes! She's just in here!' Then they show the way. If the grown-up wants to wait for a class to finish, the child will set a chair. No one has taught the children to do these things and no child is on duty to do them, it is simply how the school community works. No one is watching and the children can expect no gain from their politeness other than the proper thanks, which they get. School life outside the classroom, school life unsupervised, is often spontaneously graceful.

Into the playground during lesson time on this cold, sunny, spring Monday, an eight-year-old girl skips exuberantly. She is almost dancing across the tarmac. She is on a mission; skipping and *grinning* with the freedom of being out and about and unobserved. When she realises that she has been seen she responds only by smiling a fraction more, and without faltering or changing her speed continues skipping to the main school building. At the door she stops, composes herself, and goes in.

A small group of tiny children walks from one classroom to another through the foyer in the main school building. The convention at the school is to walk quietly and these five-year-olds were made aware of it on their first day. They remind each other earnestly, 'we're not supposed to run,' and hush each other. No teacher is in view. Sometimes a long line of six-year-olds walks by in shorts and Aertex shirts after a gym lesson in the school hall; sometimes a line of eight-year-olds walks by fully dressed on their way to the other side of the playground. Most of the children smile at visitors and some of them give the time of day. They make sure to make way if an adult needs to walk along the corridor in the opposite direction and they ask if there is enough room. The north London visitors note all this.

'They have a lot of experience of visitors, and a lot of confidence,' they say.

How these children walk, whether supervised in crocodiles or small groups, or walking on their own, is a fair expression of how they are. You rarely see children looking dejected and you almost never see them angry. There is never any shouting in the Kidlington corridors and this is so strongly established that it does not have to be enforced. Top Junior teacher Karen Errington explains, 'On the first day the children are reminded to move quietly around the school and they're shown how to line up for assembly. They know what's expected and they just do it.' (See Chapter Five.)

'The quietness is impressive,' say today's visitors. They are professionals in the field but have never seen a primary school with no noise – '*and yet it's not enforced,*' they say, wondering. However it is also crucially important to the harmonious co-existence of the 480 children that they don't get in the way of each other. The key to this benevolent orderliness is that it is in the common good. This is an extraordinarily disciplined school, and once again a word has to be redefined. Discipline usually means oppression, here it means harmony.

Noon

Most children bring packed lunches from home. From the total of about 430 Infant and Junior pupils (the other 50-odd are in the nursery school), only 60 or 70 eat a cooked midday meal, possibly because many cannot afford the £1.35 charged by the county education authority.

Children with packed lunches mostly stay in their classrooms but they may not start eating until the supervising teachers have said a short grace. Their purple, pink or blue plastic lunch boxes contain few surprises: a sandwich, an apple, a yoghurt, a drink, a biscuit, perhaps sweets or chocolate, in various combinations. Some of the picnic lunch children prefer to perch on the gymnastics forms at the corner of the school hall/dining room waiting for the school dinner children to be seated, and then find a spare place at one of the tables.

During the late morning the school hall is made into the school dining room by the addition of folding tables and chairs placed in rows and soon after midday a few children start to come in. In a short time they have become about thirty. They dispose themselves about the room; most of them sit on the floor in the corner, talking noisily. At 12.10pm Marion Trigg comes in and sits on a dining table near the large group of noisy children. She doesn't speak. The children carry on talking. After two or three minutes she says softly, 'Congratulations to that group over there for being so quiet!'

Aren't they wonderful!' – and at once all the chattering stops. This is the ploy adopted by Mr Hawkes when he says to the children coming in to assembly, 'Well done for the quiet way we're doing this!' – and it works every time. Marion Trigg starts to organise the children to go to the tables, and they find their places. Again she waits for silence, this time so she can say perhaps the best-known grace: *for what we are about to receive, may the Lord make us truly thankful*. Then she determines the order in which the children are to queue for shepherd's pie or steak and kidney, and those not yet commanded to line up for dinner sit and talk, more quietly than before.

Teachers bring sandwiches or instant noodle meals and they eat them in the staff room. Today there are biscuits brought in by a student teacher who has been doing a teaching practice in the school and is leaving. There is very often cake for someone's birthday or a celebration of a new baby or grandchild. The staff get 55 minutes to eat lunch as they are supposed to be in their classrooms five minutes before the children.

Most of the staff room conversations devolve on the children, and on logistical and organisational questions. It is surprising how much shop is talked over lunch. Teachers in general feel increasingly imposed upon, restricted and not trusted. They are watched more than they used to be and they have to account for their every action, or so it seems. They say they can't spend enough time doing pastoral work because the small latitudes they had within the school day have disappeared into the prescribed timetable and its associated, record-keeping paperwork. They worry that unless children are in a state of near-crisis they can't give the time to hear their troubles and calm them. There is some truth in this. The constraints are greater and the demands more stringent and just when one set of strictures seems to have been absorbed, another is imposed. The strength of the positive values programme at West Kidlington is that it works *within* the constraints, providing a framework for all the activities. It is the creativity of the great artist who says, 'Thank God for limitation!'

At lunchtime, all the morning class registers arrive on the office window sill and after Mrs Lobban has given tablets to any children who have to take them the office is taken over by two Year Sixes, a different pair each day. They arrive with their sandwiches and are briefed. 'A man called Steve is laying a pipe for the new outside classroom and he's expecting a call that is terribly important. Will you make sure to find him and bring him to the phone when someone rings up and asks for him?' 'Yes, Mrs Lobban.' 'You're sure you know which classroom I mean?' 'Yes.' 'Good, excellent, and if you get a moment there's these leaflets to fold. They've been counted into class piles but I want them ready to distribute to all the classrooms. Good luck, girls, enjoy yourselves!' And she's gone.

The girls perform their task with the utmost efficiency and panache. They are calm, responsible and businesslike. They soon resolve the pipe question and get on with the other jobs. Asked whether they offered to do the lunchtime office shift or were chosen, the children say they were chosen. This turns out to be only half the story. Actually many more volunteer than are needed and their teachers select those they think are the most likely to do the job well. Currently (though not always) these are all girls, since girls of ten and eleven years old are often more articulate. It is certainly true that they get the office right: everything goes like clockwork. To begin with the phone rings about every two minutes, then for a while not at all. They start to fold the leaflets, which are about the Easter programme at the local sports centre.

A girl comes by volunteering to do a job, but they have nothing to give her. 'Plants?' she wonders. ''Fraid not,' they say, 'we've already done them.' At 12.40pm two boys come to collect the class registers that were brought there at midday, and take them back to the classrooms. Steve the electrician gets another call and this time one of the girls has to go and find him, and thus the co-ordination of the gas and electricity fitting to the new auxiliary classroom can proceed towards completion on Friday, when the room will be needed for use. At one o'clock the girls hand the office back to Mrs Lobban.

1.15pm: afternoon lessons

Three neat lines of children, each headed by a class teacher, are taking different slow and deliberate tracks around the school field in the bright spring sunshine. Every so often the children stop and stare at the ground and appear to write things down (or maybe they are drawing things) on their clipboards. They are intent upon what they are doing; there is very little talking. The teachers must be asking questions because the children are following the classroom convention of putting their hands up to answer. What are they doing? 'They're detectives for Spring!' their teacher explains, 'they're looking for signs: new shoots, new grass, flowers … we're gathering evidence of Spring coming.'

3.15pm: the end of the school day

The school day starts to break up. The parents with the siblings in pushchairs return to stand waiting at the school gate, in the driveway or in the playground. The teachers stay later, putting the children's work on the wall, tidying their classrooms and preparing for the following day. On Tuesday afternoons, the massage lady will come in at about three and puts up her treatment table in the staff room, and the three or four members of staff who have booked a half-hour session with her will find things to do until their turn comes. Do other schools do this? The massage lady says very few, and those that do are all primaries. 'So much stress about these days,' she says, 'so many demands.' She draws the curtains at the large staffroom windows, turns on the table lamps, turns off the ceiling lights, and greets her first client. 'This is your half-hour, let's get rid of all the aches.' An oasis.

5.00pm: winding up

Many of Alex Vincent's tasks have to wait until there are no pupils left in the school. Painting is an obvious one, fixing classroom windows another, then there are unblocking lavatories and polishing floors, including the big wooden one in the school hall/gymnasium, which has to be done twice a week. He also has to take out the rubbish from the kitchens and classrooms and set everywhere up shipshape again for tomorrow's school. He works alongside the cleaning ladies but they have something of an advantage in that they can start their tasks while the children are going home. They set to work vacuuming the corridors and the library, leaving the classrooms until the school is finally empty again.

For Neil Hawkes, the last week of term is far from relaxing. There are still important meetings to conduct, things to sort out for next term, and all of it with people who are winding down. The departure of the children at the end of their school day was simply a signal for the beginning of a different stage of his own, different meetings, more paperwork, in a quieter atmosphere. He says he doesn't like the school all that much when the children aren't there. The teachers who can take their marking work home do so. At about 6.30pm, Alex Vincent, if he complains enough, may be able to lock up and go home.

THE KIDLINGTON BLUEPRINT

As parents, you can take a leaf out of the Kidlington teachers' book. Try for positive thinking all the time. The ordinary and everyday provide constant opportunities for observation and for practising the positive values programme.

- When the children of West Kidlington School run the office at lunchtime they demonstrate what they have learned as they operate the switchboard and welcome and direct visitors. First and foremost they are responsible. They are also considerate, sensitive and polite.

- The children who play so well together at break time are learning their social lessons against a backdrop of honourable, proper behaviour.

- The child who skipped across the playground added to the world's store of gaiety. Allow yourself the joy of watching and sharing the fun of the moment.

At home these principles can be applied subtly.

- When playing with your children you can introduce your value word from time to time, just to keep it in view.

- When you read their bedtime story soften the lighting and ask for their calm and focussed attention on the tale and its characters. There is probably no need to keep mentioning value words at story time, however. The event is profoundly special and the story will have its own power.

- When you are out and about with your children, perhaps at the supermarket or walking in the park, comment on the joyful things. A friendly dog, a smiling old lady, a tree in spring blossom or autumn colour, the polite behaviour of a child, a helpful shop assistant, are all life-affirming elements that can be pointed out and act as a beautiful antidote to the more general diet of criticism and gloom.

As always, lightness of touch is the key.

CHAPTER 3

How it's Done

W HEN IT WAS DECIDED TO START A QUIET REVOLUTION BY PLACING values centre stage at West Kidlington school there was (by definition) no structured way of doing it, no existing plan, and no single text book or scheme of work to provide the materials. There was only a conviction that positive values should be at the heart of all the school activities whether academic or social. The task contained many practical problems, not least the multi-faith character of schools in the United Kingdom. None of the traditional religions would suit all the staff and children and not offend any of the parents, indeed not every child or family – or even West Kidlington teacher – believes in a deity. However, it was seen that certain positive concepts are timeless and irrefutable whatever people believe or don't believe, and that they should be considered for use in depth with all age groups. Linda Heppenstall says, 'The good rules have lasted because they work,' and on this there was consensus.

Identifying the key values

Linda Heppenstall was asked to produce 22 key values, one for each month of a two-year cycle. Only August is missed out of the West Kidlington values year, for although schools have long holidays, term times include some part of all the other months. Thus there are 22 peerless building blocks for the lives of all the children and the adults at the school, 22 values such as love and truth and hope, which are examined and re-examined and their outcomes in terms of behaviour and perception assessed. This structure for living could hardly be stronger. Such an emphasis is like building a house on firm foundations, eating only wholesome food, absorbing enough sunshine but not too much – any of the obvious similes will do. *The good rules have lasted because they work*. This is the basis of the Kidlington blueprint and the foundation of the Quiet Revolution.

The theme words that mark out the months at West Kidlington were developed slowly over a period of a year, and refined over a second year. Much of the early work was done by Linda Heppenstall and her starting points for the children were:

- Living a better life.

- Being a better person.

- Being happier with who you are.

- Understanding who you are.

Linda Heppenstall says that when Neil Hawkes began introducing values into assemblies he asked the teachers to go back to their rooms and continue working on the value words with their pupils. When they did so, they quickly discovered that they wanted at least one extra session a week for the task. The concepts were so strong, so rich in potential, and so interesting to the children, that they deserved more exploration. Of course, this work had to be at the right level for the individual year groups. So that everyone on the staff could develop the themes for the needs of their own classes Linda Heppenstall gave each teacher a sheet of paper with a grid on it to show their lesson plans. She asked them to describe the structure of their lessons and what they had used to illustrate the concepts.

Linda Heppenstall For a starting point for the teachers, and to get the children to think more about using values for themselves I used the *Living Values** books. Then the teachers found their own stories and devised their own worksheets, all of which went into a sort of bank we were setting up. For the first two years the teachers invented all their values lessons and when there was enough material in a proper, coherent form for people to draw on, we started to be able to give those lessons back to them. At last there was no need to find new material. All the time they were working on it and we were putting material into the bank I always said, if you find anything better let me know, this is just to get it started. They did a huge amount of work. It took some badgering to get it all in, and of course it had to slow down at times like Christmas or when we were being inspected. It took ages! I think it was a wonderful effort.

* *Living Values* books are published by UNICEF.

This wonderful effort was undertaken willingly by the West Kidlington teaching staff because they found it entirely engaging and because when they started to work on the positive values programme with the children they found it to be enriching at every level. Here are the values.

quality	*co-operation*
unity	*understanding*
peace	*honesty*
happiness	*appreciation*
hope	*courage*
patience	*love*
caring	*friendship*
humility	*thoughtfulness*
simplicity	*tolerance*
trust	*responsibility*
freedom	*respect*

Developing the values programme

The discussion of complex, abstract concepts is not something usually associated with young children and yet it turns out that five-year-olds are indeed able to consider quite complicated hypothetical situations. An example of this is offered by the conversations on 'Who is your friend?', which are undertaken in depth by Year One children at a class conversation called circle time, when the children sit on the floor and the talk is led by their teacher. The questions begin, 'Who is your friend?', 'What do you like about your friend?' and 'What do you enjoy doing with your friend?' In later years, they move to more complicated problems such as, 'What if your friend asked you to do something you didn't want to do, would they still be your friend?' and ultimately the very taxing, 'What if your friend said they wouldn't be your friend if you didn't do the thing you didn't want to do, would you do it then?' The example they use is emotive indeed: smoking. 'What if your friend said they wouldn't be your friend if you didn't share their cigarette?'

For the mechanics within the education hierarchy this exercise has to be justified on technical grounds. It can easily be done on grounds of developing sophisticated levels of articulacy, handling difficult problems and considering the consequences of action. The technical skills are invaluable, and are much enhanced in pursuit of questions, which are fascinating to the children. Many school inspectors, however, recognise the critical importance of spiritual development. Their Framework for Inspection says:

> 'Spiritual development relates to that aspect of inner life through which pupils acquire insights into their personal existence, which are of enduring worth. It is characterised by reflection, the attribution of meaning to experience, valuing a non-material dimension to life, and intimations of an enduring reality.
> "Spiritual" is not synonymous with "religious"; all areas of the curriculum may contribute to pupils' spiritual development.'

However, although some inspectors recognise such delicate, intangible, and in the understanding of West Kidlington Primary School, crucial elements/qualities, they are nevertheless by definition intangible and unmarkable and they don't get you a job. They therefore form no part of the official assessment of schools and of the state of the nation's children. Yet, as far as parents, teachers and children are concerned, they are pivotally important.

The mental exercise on moral questions was found to be just as interesting for the teachers and all of them say they enjoyed it. This too is remarkable, for they have been under great pressure to work only for objectives such as performance targets and test results, and are under ever-increasing obligations to put in extra time on tasks such as record-keeping. The fact that they not only involved themselves in the substantial additional effort of building up the values programme and generating the materials for it, but also said they enjoyed doing so, could be regarded as something of a miracle.

The programme did not spring fully formed from the mind of any one person. Even now it is still evolving. The staff worked especially hard on it for the first two years. There were many influences and sources, and the abstract, idealistic questions are constantly reconsidered in the light of everyday experience. Most of the teachers are also parents and have had to find practical solutions to the problems and questions brought by their children without any touchstone from which to do it. Thus they were practised at navigating complicated matters, and at finding pragmatic answers, and came to the task of creating a formal yet flexible values structure from a background of practical experience but usually little philosophical training.

Defining spirituality

Among the first of the problems was to arrive at an acceptable definition of spirituality. The word is trapped in associations with formal religions and high-flown edicts. This is Mark Halstead's (Reader in Education at Plymouth University) definition:

> 'Spirituality can be thought of as our personal inner world of thoughts and feelings. A world that is real, in the sense that it is our consciousness but cannot be seen. Only the results of our thoughts and feelings can be seen, in the form of actions, which create the material world of objects such as clothes, cars and so on.'

Neil Hawkes qualifies this by noting that in the more advanced spiritual studies, thoughts and feelings are seen as the route to a higher elevation where there are neither. For the purposes of the work being done with the children at West Kidlington School, however, it is the definition currently in use. The practice and habit of observing and evaluating is one that enables different conclusions to be made, from which adjustments in behaviour can follow. It is an invaluable discipline that develops the capacity for objective observation and slows down action to the point where it can be considered, planned and afterwards assessed, and not just be reactive and emotional. By this means it is possible that the headstrong and violent behaviour associated with sudden reaction could disappear entirely. Certainly it is what the great spiritual teachers recommend, the Dalai Lama among them. In *Ancient Wisdom, Modern World* he says, 'The more we succeed in transforming our hearts and minds through cultivating spiritual qualities, the better able we will be to cope with adversity and the greater the likelihood that our actions will be ethically wholesome.'

A place for children

The children are given the tools with which they can clearly see their own part in the social world in which they live and their own contribution to its harmony. They are given them in such a way that they can make the necessary adjustments to their lives without feeling that if they have behaved inappropriately they have failed. They can adjust from a position of strength and self-esteem. They can say to themselves dispassionately, this course of action didn't work, then how shall I do it differently? How can I put it right?

The foundation is this: the children of West Kidlington School stand straight with the world, they know who they are, and they know that they are valuable (this has nothing to do with ego). From this point they can make choices, they can do a great many things. The term self-esteem currently in constant use is one they don't need to worry about since they have it already. The self that is esteemed can be defined: the best of themselves is admirable, less happy aspects are allowed or persuaded to disappear, leaving the virtuous core of the child intact.

Running parallel with the evolution of the classroom materials and the daily discipline of reflection for the school either as a whole or in separate classes was a strong feeling that the teachers needed some guidelines too. The logic of the values programme determines that demands made upon children must not be greater than those made upon adults. The teachers needed their own structure to support their own aspirations, and after thought and discussion they arrived at a definition of the effort they felt they must make for themselves. Here is a summary, and it is equally applicable to home life as it is to the school.

The values programme tool kit

Step 1: have a clear understanding of what spirituality means

Begin to develop an understanding of your inner world of thoughts, feelings and emotions. This is your spiritual world. A clear understanding of your own spirit will enable you to develop an understanding of the concept of spirituality, which is at the heart of values education.

What is spirituality?

- We are beings made up of body and spirit. We are aware of our bodies and a moment's thought will make us similarly aware that we are conscious beings, with ideas and powerful emotions. They are the essence of our spiritual world – of spirituality.

- We can think of ways to develop the physical body or the intellectual mind, but what about the spirit? If the spirit is not developed we grow into incomplete adults in just the same way as if the body and mind are not developed we will not be able to lead full and contented lives.

- How can we begin to understand what our spirit is? Imagine a delicious chocolate with an almond centre. The wrapping is like the body, attractive and eye-catching. The chocolate represents the conscious mind, and at the centre the nut, or nugget, is the same for everyone. It is the source of qualities and virtues such as love, trust, truth and peace: it is the *higher self*. It needs to be nurtured to affect the quality of our own and other people's lives.

- We can appreciate that each of us has a spirit. It is possible to say, 'I don't know your name but I recognise who you are,' as an acknowledgement of something we all have and can all share, the higher self, the spirit. It is within each of us and it accepts that we are more than the everyday roles we play such as husband, wife, parent or teacher.

Step 2: get to know your spiritual self

Quiet reflection is the route. Give yourself time to be with yourself and begin to explore your spiritual being by sitting quietly and focusing on aspects of yourself that create good feelings. Make sure to create thoughts and images that do not lead to a critical frame of mind. If negative thoughts occur to you, acknowledge them and ask them to move on so you can concentrate on positive ones.

Then hold meetings with yourself.

- Give yourself regular, quiet, reflective times to put you in touch with your spiritual self, create well-being and help you to be in control of your life.

- During reflection, consider qualities such as humility, respect, responsibility and love. What do they mean? Are you aware of them within yourself? They may be hidden. Over time you will reach your higher self, and know and appreciate your spiritual identity. The method is simple and only needs a commitment to put aside a regular time for practice. The concepts can be explored in *Values for a Better World*.

Step 3: have a desire to grow spiritually

Getting to know yourself is hard work, it is a lifetime's journey. *Be on that journey*. The rewards are enormous as you become more objectively self-aware and self-confident. If you teach, you will find that your teaching will improve and be less stressful as you concentrate on the positive rather than beating yourself up for perceived failures. Learn to praise yourself!

When you are on this journey, you consciously and unconsciously begin to show your inner self, your best self. You become a model for others, an example, and children recognise and respond to it. For instance, as you develop the quality of respect within yourself you may see your children differently, as equal beings sharing a learning experience with you. They will notice and respond with respect.

The more you raise your inner, spiritual qualities, the more you will raise the self-respect and self-esteem of children and adults around you. This follows when you appreciate your children, you are honest with them, and you trust them. Without self-esteem there is no learning progress.

Step 4: communicate with others on a spiritual level

As you become more aware of your spiritual self you will find you are more likely to communicate with others spiritually. You begin to see people at a level not dominated by appearance. You are less likely to think of people from the viewpoint of your own selfish ego.

How do people communicate?
Usually at three points:

- Through appearance (nice but transient).
- Through personality/emotion (can be very nice but can also be painful).
- Spiritually. This is what we really want: a deeper, spiritual connection with unconditional love and acceptance. When you communicate with people at this level it will be evident in everything you do and say, manifest in your interactions and your relationships.

It is important to communicate with children spiritually too. You will find that they respond appropriately without realising why. They will have respect for you. If you are a teacher, they will consider you to be a good teacher, and you will find the job of teaching becomes easier and more fulfilling.

Step 5: actively teach others

Plan to develop your children's ability on all the steps given up to now. Emphasise:

- Stillness, calm and reflection.

- Monthly values, through well-planned assemblies, class lessons and circle time (if you are a teacher) and stories that penetrate deep layers of human experience and discussion of values, both at home and at school.

- The children's spiritual core.

Conclusion

Developing the spiritual climate of home and school for values education requires total commitment. In a school, it follows that the head teacher must model values education for the staff, and the school as a whole must walk its talk. Children are quick to spot inconsistencies. Do not expect behaviour from a child that you are not prepared to offer yourself.

If you are dedicated to raising standards you cannot ignore spiritual development. And if you work on that, you are committed to developing the whole individual, child or adult.

The school is a microcosm of the world. What is created in school today can provide a glimpse of how our world can be tomorrow.

The values programme in practice

With the values programme in place, the staff at West Kidlington School find that they like the ethos of honest hard work, the parents like their motivated, happy children and the children like the clarity and security of shared values. The whole school works well, and the teachers say again and again how much the programme has enhanced and simplified the work in the school and also their own lives. In response to questions about the work put into devising the 22 words, they say that it was time-consuming but engrossing and has made their lives much easier. It is quite simply easier for everyone within the school community to be working from the same point outwards, and for that central point to be seen to be energising and positive. It makes life clear, and takes away the fuzzy edges. This summary of what adults must offer to children is informally agreed in the West Kidlington staff room.

Consistency of approach

So children are secure.

So children can't play off one adult against another, e.g. 'Miss Jones lets us do that.'

So the adult world is safe and honourable, and seen to be so.

Kindness

Based on the loving appraisal of the individual needs of each child so the children are nourished by a loving environment.

Fair dealing

No bias towards particular children or adults: children have a strong sense of fair play.

Strength

No prevarication or ambiguity. Straightforward, simple guidelines create security.

Truthfulness

Put kindly, the honest answer is the best, creates trust.

Trustworthiness

Promises made to children must be kept, confidences maintained.

Implementing the values programme

In addition to these precepts, there are many helpful notes from Neil Hawkes and at staff meetings the values programme and its logistics are constantly under review. With a whole school ethos as strong and demanding as this there must be constant attention, both to the larger cause and the fine detail. Neil Hawkes offers the following pointers as practical guidelines for teaching the values programme:

- As values are introduced in assemblies each month, children get familiar with the language and the ideas.

- Lots of basic training is needed especially in the early years – manners, routines, picking up the positive and giving praise when children show respect, caring, etc.

- Have high expectations, set clear boundaries: the foundations of good values require good discipline.

- Aim for a calm, reflective atmosphere, which facilitates contemplation. Then children get to know themselves better and develop a sense of responsibility for their own lives and happiness.

- At the start of the year decide your own class rules – let all the children contribute. Rules made in this way will become the children's own rules, based on values such as respect for people and property. This develops responsibility.

- Take opportunities in the curriculum to discuss values as they arise naturally, e.g. in history or literature.

- Explore the values work and present in class assemblies.

- Remember to live the values. We teach best by being role models.

This effort in its totality could be compared with setting up a beautiful garden, putting in healthy plants, using only natural compost, watering just enough, and letting nature and sunshine do their work. Thought must be put into planning the garden. It must be watched carefully but not inter-fered with too much. It must be fed organically at the right time and although the gardener must be constantly watchful it is not necessary to be constantly active, as the garden if properly set up and fed will grow beau-tifully from nature alone. Over-pruning is harmful, and pruning young plants will damage them irrevocably, so pruning must be done carefully and only at the right time. If all these kind rules are followed the garden will blossom and flourish, and it will appear to have done it all by itself. As the colours change with the seasons, the plants will always harmonise with each other. When to intervene and when not to intervene will be clear to the gardener who, having set it all up in a healthy and thoughtful way, will know that much the best way to get the garden to grow is to let it do it by itself.

This offers an exact parallel with the nurturing of young children, the ideal situation being this, that they be given the conditions in which to flourish and then as far as possible left to grow unhindered. The gardener, of course, is any adult, teacher, parent, guardian or carer, with the skill, commitment and love to do the work of the garden. It is worth noting that the parents of West Kidlington pupils are often deeply affected by this effort and find that their lives are also flourishing in unexpected ways (see Chapter Seven).

Incorporating the values programme
into lesson plans

The theme concept is used academically at the school in two ways: first in the Spiritual, Moral, Social and Cultural (SMSC) lessons, which are focused wholly upon it, and second as an idea that occurs within general subjects. Integrated into general lessons the positive value word will have greater or lesser relevance according to the subject and it will be clear that teachers can build the words into arts subjects more easily than into science and maths. During the month of respect, for example, a teacher might ask the class in a history lesson to consider whether King Henry VIII showed respect to his wives. But it is more difficult to see how respect could be fitted into the study of size and volume, or the life-cycle of the butterfly. More of this in the next chapter. (The charts that show how it works are in the appendix.)

Simply, the words are used during the ordinary school day as often as possible. This includes the daily process of socialisation, whether between generations or in the essential development of relationships between the children. For parents and families the habit of repeating positive concepts is similarly strengthening, helping to unite and harmonise and maintain the focus on simple joyful appreciation. The outside world is notoriously fond of emphasising gloom and fear at the expense of optimism and constructiveness but the antidote is surprisingly easy to find. The dock leaf always grows next to the nettle.

Happiness in Year One

Many adults are amazed that the values concepts are taken into the first year primary classes and yet, as we have seen, the ability of the five-year-olds to consider complex questions is profound. They often have a very clear vision on moral questions and offer it confidently in discussions. They talk about the concepts during a special conversation lesson called circle time, when they sit in a circle and a topic is introduced, usually a song is sung, then the word comes under the spotlight. The word happiness, for Year Ones, is defined for whoever is teaching them as a good feeling. The note for teachers defines it a little more closely:

> *Teacher Understanding*: if sought from outside sources (wealth, material possessions, status, relationships) happiness is temporary. Lasting happiness is a state of contentment within – not needing to be fed by outside wants.

The song suggested for the Year One children is *If you want to be happy* and the notes offer ideas for discussion: 'Talk about things that make us feel happy.' This topic first came up during an autumn term, so many of the children's suggestions for happiness were seasonal. They said, 'my birthday', 'making a snowman', 'Christmas', 'cuddling my rabbit', 'going on a picnic'. There was talk about these happy occasions and activities, then the conversation became more abstract. The question put to the children was, 'How can we make other people happy?'

From this point the ideas in such a discussion are more demanding. Once the groundwork has been carefully laid, however, the talk usually becomes quite animated, as it did on the day the topic was introduced. The question was answered first by the word friendship. If we are kind and share things with others it gives us a good, happy feeling inside, the record says. It was noticed that happiness came from giving something not necessarily material, and observing the effect of the gift on the recipient. This was really enough for such a young group and had shifted the conversation very well from the concrete to the abstract. But just to finish off the lesson, the teacher made the point that unhappy feelings could always be taken to a caring adult, such as a parent, grandparent or teacher, and did not get better by being hidden inside.

Thus the ideal and the practical outcomes of proper behaviour were demonstrated, the abstract and the concrete discussed, and some of the basic foundation ideas for a world based on observation and harmonious behaviour were presented and investigated in a comprehensible form. The children were also shown that there were obvious benefits for givers of proper gifts, the nice warm feeling that comes from a kind action being top of the list. And finally, as a safety measure, the teacher made it clear that unhappy feelings would always be the business of an adult somewhere, who would do their best to soothe and disperse them.

Happiness in Year Two

Year Twos move up a peg. They are asked 'What makes you happy?' and invited to distinguish between happy feelings created by things that are exciting, unusual and so on, and feelings that are deeper and more long-lasting. Here are some of their observations, written one December day in the run-up to Christmas, inside the outline of a big smiley face.

I feel happy when I hug my mum.

I feel happy when I do good work.

I feel happy when I think of Jesus.

I feel happy because it is Christmas.

I feel happy because I lick [like?] food.

I feel happy because Jesus is born.

Happiness in Year Three

Year Threes sit down for their circle time and are invited to change places if they have had a happy experience during the year, then change again if they have had an unhappy experience. This necessitates a lot of moving and emphasises the constant presence of both sides of the happiness coin. The next game is to say in turn 'I feel happy when …' and the one after that goes 'I make someone happy when …'. In pairs, the children talk about how they can make other people happy, and also set out to discover what makes them both happy.

Happiness in Year Four

Eight-year-olds consider whether they need others to make them happy, and whether they know how to create happiness in themselves and in others. By this time they are being set written work of some complexity. The subject for writing is 'What makes me feel happy – is it something outside myself, or something I can help control?'

Happiness – and honesty – in Year Five

The level of abstract thinking intensifies the further up the age range they go, so that Year Fives are invited to look at the environment and identify things that make them happy, then think of a happy colour and say why it is a happy colour. At its first outing this brought:

'My family makes me happy because they are caring. My friends make me happy by playing with me. When we go on holiday it makes me happy because the whole family is together and we have great fun. My birthday makes me happy because it is my special day.'

'My favourite colour is yellow because it is the colour of the blazing sun and the tropical pineapple, the mouth-watering banana ice cream, the smooth hot sand and the sweet yellow chicks. When I think of yellow I am happy because it reminds me of these things.'

One of the compositions saved in the teacher reference folder tells of a walk in the park with a favourite doll, seeing a poor child drop her doll and break it, and giving the favourite doll to the child who had suffered the loss, in order to comfort her. It ends: 'Lisa said do not cry you can have my doll the girl said thankyou thankyou.' It is a retelling of the story *Nathalie's Doll*, from *Education in Human Values* by June Auton, a key text in the evolution and practice of the West Kidlington values programme. Among the Activity Choices offered at the end of the story and discussion are: make a frieze of happy/sad faces, draw a picture that conveys 'Happiness', write sentences which begin, 'Happiness is …'. This work generated the quoted composition.

Another series of happiness questions for Year Five goes:

Discuss when we feel happy/sad:

- What do we feel like doing when we are happy?
- Can we feel happy for the successes of others?
- Is happiness a result of what we think or feel?
- Can we change the way we view things – look at things another way?
- Where do feelings of happiness/sadness come from?
- How do you feel when you make others happy?

Year Five is the responsibility of Linda Heppenstall, and it was one of her classes I observed for the second feature about West Kidlington School that I wrote for the *Times Educational Supplement*. The word of the moment was honesty and the class considered the consequences of the wolf-crying tendency of Matilda in Hilaire Belloc's eponymous poem. We may recall that Matilda likes to shout 'fire!' and get the fire brigade out, so is not believed when a real fire starts but is burnt to a cinder instead. 'What does honesty mean?' was the first question. Children spoke of telling the truth, owning up to things, and feeling bad about doing something wrong until owning up about it put it right.

Richard said he wanted to talk about something that had happened during the week, and introduced for public examination an incident which initially showed him in a poor light but from which he had been able to recover himself. The conversation was impressive for several reasons. Richard clearly still had doubts about what had happened, he had not quite resolved in his mind whether the incident could have been handled differently, he wanted his classmates to help him and he was able to offer his dilemma for consideration. That the school develops the confidence for such openness is one of its greatest strengths. The class analysed the question put by an individual member of it, neither making capital from his behaviour nor scoring points for themselves, but considering action and consequence and reaching careful, almost dispassionate judgements. Once again, the children are put in charge of their own decision-making and made responsible for their own behaviour in a supported way that is simultaneously gentle and strong.

Although it is true that this makes great demands on the children it could be said that real irresponsibility in adults is when they do not help their children to develop self-responsibility. By this means dependency and fear are created, with their uncomfortable resulting symptoms such as defensiveness and showing-off. Another great irresponsibility in adults is to grant self-responsibility inappropriately to children, placing them in situations they cannot handle.

At West Kidlington, children are guided and given the tools with which to make decisions, and the decisions and their consequences are considered in a safe and supportive way. They are shown how to see their part in the totality, their proper place in the community. They are practised in asking themselves the question, 'How do I live in the world so that I get what I want from it, while remaining in harmony with the rest of my community?' Perhaps acquiring the tools to arrive at this invaluable wisdom could be likened to being taught to swim with proper strokes, breathing properly, building up the strength of the arms and legs and lungs, so as to be able to swim in any waters. If the technique is not properly learned the swimmer may get by in simple situations but they will not be able to cope with difficult ones.

The problem was this: Richard had taken a football without asking and hidden it in his locker because a bigger boy with whom he had been playing had kicked him. Richard was not sure if he could have handled it differently: he had not been able to see another course of action at the time. The incident was referred to the class for investigation without comment or criticism from Linda Heppenstall and the children looked at many different avenues that Richard could have taken.

'You could have told Miss Robinson.'

'You should have kicked him back!'

'That boy always kicks people, you should have told Miss.'

'Yeah, he kicks everybody all the time because he's bigger.'

'I'd have made him give it back!' – 'How?' – 'Just telling him.' – 'Wouldn't work.'

'I would have taken it away from him.'

None of the suggestions was found to be efficacious or appropriate. The boy who kicked was too big to be challenged but it was not thought quite right to involve the teacher in it.

'But when you put the football away, no one could play football,' observed Mrs Heppenstall, 'and you couldn't play football either. What did you do for the rest of break time, Richard?' The boy said he had found something else to do that had been just as good, but whatever it was, it was clear to himself and everyone listening that it had been a poor substitute. The hidden football had eaten away at the back of his mind until two or three days later he had returned it to the teacher. 'And what did Miss Robinson say when you took the football back, Richard?', asked Mrs Heppenstall. 'She said, "thank you for being honest!"', said Richard.

The children had spent some time on this discussion and although none of them had come up with a solution to the problem of dealing with the boy who kicked, they had considered various avenues of action and seen why they would not work. For Richard to kick the boy back would start a fight, and the other was bigger and stronger. Also kicking and hitting are not allowed at the school. Telling teacher probably wouldn't work because the boy would be likely to take it out on Richard later. The important thing for Richard was that he had not liked how he felt with the football hidden in his locker. He had known that it would have to be given back, he could see that hiding it stopped him and the other children from playing, and he had restored it.

The critically important thing for Richard and for the rest of the children was that having worked out his own proper solution he had been thanked for it. The word of the month was honesty, he had behaved honestly, and he had been supported in his effort. Such faith in the children's capacity for understanding and for reaching the proper conclusion and acting upon it is shown to bring great rewards. Richard saw that if he acted in accordance with his best self he would not only feel right but also be endorsed in his proper behaviour. Thus his best self was strengthened and his inner knowledge of how to do things was reaffirmed.

The other children, by participating in his dilemma, saw the outcome from their own individual points of view. They examined several options in great detail – incidentally a scientific process. (People who prefer to have classroom work justified on grounds of learning technical skills can take heart from noting the careful consideration of the processes of cause and effect, stimulus and result, which take place in the values lessons.) Finally when the children were asked for a piece of written work, eleven-year old Alex brought in the honesty rap.

> Being honest is the right thing to do,
> Being honest with your friends and honest with you,
> So brighten up and be the best,
> If you work on it you'll be better than the rest.
> Honesty is a real nice feeling,
> Tell the truth and you'll hit the ceiling,
> Tell a lie and you'll regret it,
> It's no good saying, 'I never did it.'
> How do you feel when you tell a lie?
> Doesn't it make you want to die?
> Stealing is a bad thing to do,
> We don't do it, why should you?
> Do what's right and you will see,
> Be honest, and happy is what you'll be.

All of this clearly demonstrates Neil Hawkes' observation that during their formative years children are learning the building blocks for life so that, 'Later on, when they find themselves in difficult situations, they don't just bale out. Hopefully this foundation will last them for all of their lives.'

Happiness in Year Six

By Year Six, the discussion on happiness has moved to world religions, their differences and similarities, and is well on the way towards the concept that happiness comes from within. It is observed that the practice of meditation helps Buddhists to find inner contentment, to see themselves as separate from their physical wants, to reflect on their god-like qualities and find true happiness. Here is a sample essay by one of the children.

Meditation

Buddhist people meditate all the time throughout their lives. They focus on one thing for hours. Meditating is just like praying and speaking to god. Sometimes people think they're something else. They have to relax their bodies they have to think and concentrate until they can see a picture in their minds of what they are concentrating on or until they've cleared their minds and they can see what happiness really is. The main reason why they meditate is so they can clear their minds.

The Blue Band Monitors

Lessons and circle time are part of the values effort, which actually takes place throughout the school day. It affects social interaction hugely. The complexity of relationships between the West Kidlington school children is very great. As they get higher up the school many pupils take on responsibilities which are traditionally alienating, such as monitoring the playground behaviour. All the children have responsibility for their own playground behaviour but some of the older children volunteer to monitor it. They do so in groups, two or three sessions every week, on a rota. The playground, that great seedbed for social life, is watched over by some of the Year Sixes, who wear distinguishing blue bands, and once again the quality of the activity has to be carefully defined.

This watching is in no way like the school prefect system of old, with children acting as honorary beaks with a remit to stitch you up. The concern at West Kidlington is to maintain harmonious play and prevent physical injury and it is fairly rare for any situation to reach the point of involving a teacher. Of course, there is always a teacher on duty in the playground at break times – but only one. The Blue Band children who assist them act, in the words of their brief, as 'eyes and ears for the teachers'. They do this conscientiously. The school inspectors said, 'Playtimes and lunchtimes are lively, with children of different ages playing happily together. The older children carry out their extra responsibilities ... with care, competence and good humour.'

Good humour is always necessary, more or less always maintained, and sometimes especially well rewarded. The deputy head told a good tale: he had separated two boys who were fighting. It goes without saying that fighting is not allowed. The teacher took the boys indoors to speak to them about it. 'When should you have stopped this argument?' he asked the boys. 'I shouldn't have told him I was better at doing a yo yo than him,' replied the first boy. 'And I shouldn't have strangled him,' admitted the second.

However, the no fighting rule is generally observed. The Blue Band Monitors are very keen on it. The rules of play include no sticks, no hard balls and no bullying. (The children can play football in the play-ground with soft balls; the plastic-covered ones are for the playing field.) Among the important monitoring duties is watching the gates to make sure the smallest children don't run out into the road. It is only a side road but still a serious consideration and the Blue Band children take it seriously. They are briefed to be reasonable, not bossy, and they must always try to resolve situations by asking for different behaviour. They understand that if they volunteer for blue band duty they will have to maintain their com-mitment to it for a term. Though the rota is flexible enough for the duties to fall only one or two days a week, and they only have to perform them at lunchtime and not during the mid-morning break, it is none the less an important part of the acceptance of responsibility. The children understand they won't be able to duck out of it halfway through the term.

When one of the Blue Band teams outlined its tasks, Sam began by remarking that they didn't really have much to do on their playground duty because, 'We're supposed to stop people being horrible to people, but they aren't often horrible anyway. When it happens we just ask them to stop, and they do.' The monitors observed that the Infants took much more notice of them than the Juniors; indeed that approaching Infants even very gently, as they have been taught, can be enough to frighten them. 'Once I went to an Infant who threw a stone and he started to shake,' said a girl, 'so I said, it's all right, we're not telling you off! The Infants get frightened, but it was OK in the end.' Another monitor said that when she told off a boy for running directly across the school field (not using the track) he started crying. The monitors find this response upsetting and always try to calm things down. It is unusual for them to have to involve a teacher.

'There are eight monitors on the playground now,' they explained. 'We had to work out how many to have. That means the gates are watched and there are some people extra for looking at behaviour. If you're not doing your job properly they'll ask you to stop – it's not often, but sometimes if people start getting bossy it could lead to bullying and then they'd have to go.'

The children say there are sometimes sticky moments but they are always able to resolve them. Once when a monitor asked a boy to stop playing with a plastic ball [a large, hard football] at lunchtime, on the grounds that people could get hurt by it, the boy cried and ran away, the monitor set off to talk to him and found him with a gang. 'I was scared at first,' said the monitor, 'but I spent ten minutes explaining what a monitor does, and they were all right in the end.' She thought for a moment. 'We have to set an example,' she said, and paused for another moment. 'Grave responsibility, isn't it?'

The social side is also interesting for them: to begin with, when children volunteer for Blue Band duty their friends sometimes say they won't play with them any more – but they find that they soon want to join up themselves. One of the girls observed, 'You don't have to be a monitor to do what a monitor does. It's common sense really.' The children say they bring a teacher in on the rare occurrences of bullying or being ignored when they ask for changed behaviour, and they pay the most attention to the Infants. They are all far more concerned about the tiny children than they are about the fabric of the school; indeed, the Infants are at the top of their list of priorities. They have been taught this: their first concern is the safety of other children.

In and out of the playground, one of the differences of this school community that is most frequently commented upon by the parents is how well the children support each other. It was also mentioned in the official report of the Ofsted school inspectors, who are trained and briefed to look much more keenly at academic test results than at the fine tuning of sensitive behaviour, and who commented on it in connection with their many compliments for general behaviour. 'The high quality of relationships in the school and the excellent behaviour of pupils are evidence of the extremely effective provision for the moral and social development brought about through the consistent and successful application of the values policy.' This mutual support is perceived to be exceptionally well developed and is a source of great strength not only for the individual children but also for the school as a whole. Thus it is visible to the inspectors who are not really supposed to be looking for it and who comment like all other visitors to the school on the wonderfully calm and happy atmosphere. This speaks well for the outward manifestations of the values programme and augurs well for the future strength of at least some local communities.

The School Council

Children take another influential role when they join the School Council, a body that meets twice a week to talk about day-to-day matters such as tidy cloakrooms, which they inspect and award stickers for. Good behaviour, smiling and being good-humoured are also awarded congratulation stickers at a special assembly (see Chapter Five). In making these awards the children are recognising the benefit to the school community of harmonious behaviour. Members of the Council are elected within their classes by their classmates, and remain in place for about a year. They must be at least Year Three.

Council members watch for people being kind, so that they can reward them, and they say their guiding principle is that, 'Everyone should learn to respect each other, respect the values, and be peaceful and thoughtful.' The environmental group within the Council pays particular attention to the school pond. 'Now it's full of *nature*!' said eight-year-old councillor Clare enthusiastically, moderating the observation to explain that it had actually been full of nature before they started clearing the long grass but that now you could see it. Darren said they had help from the mums, and the pond group had organised the working parties into groups that ensured no one got hurt.

The School Council has reorganised itself to be less hierarchical and more accessible, both at its own meetings and in relation to the rest of the school. 'We decided not to have a chair,' they explained, 'we're all equal, we'll discuss things, no one's more important than anyone else.' Of their school responsibilities they say, 'The children find trust in us. We get both sides of stories.' Throughout the explanation of their function the Council members sprinkle pointers as to how they regulate themselves. You must forgive and forget; you can have an argument but you must make it up; if something goes wrong you have to work out where it started and put it right (and you might have to go back weeks!) – are among them.

Members of the School Council often mention the value words in the context of their efforts, which they recognise are demanding. 'It's a lot of work,' they say, 'but we enjoy it.' Parents regard the workings of the Council as beneficial to members and to the school as a whole. They say that the children take responsibility and exercise it with care. Parents also note that the smaller children are happy to pay attention to children who are near to them in age, and have the further benefit of seeing pupils not much older than themselves brought in to be instrumental in the decision-making and running of the school.

The values programme and parent involvement

Parents are told the current value word through *Dolphin News*, the school newsletter, and the words and the programme come under discussion at parent–teacher meetings, which are generally well attended. Some of the parents remark on changes of behaviour wrought by the values concepts. Mrs Arekalian, a governor who helps in the school with reading, has two children there and also runs the school gardening club, reported that throughout the month of respect her son miraculously offered to wash up after the evening meal practically every night. 'It was wonderful!' she said. The fact that the offers stopped when the month was over was felt to be a good thing rather than a bad one since such virtue cannot be expected to last at a constant level, especially when there's another value to work on. Children absorb the idea and move on. The idea and its implications and consequent actions remain part of their young lives, and many parents acknowledge that there cannot be constantly visible results. However, in the same way that eating a wholesome dinner builds strong bone and tissue for future use, so the values lessons strengthen the character and sharpen the perceptions of the children for the rest of their lives. The values lessons are the touchstone, the backbone, the core, from which the world in its variety can be viewed.

Parent-teacher meetings usually focus on the values work and parents are kept informed, as they would be in any school, of new work, new ideas, curriculum changes, new government requirements and changes within the school structure. Often they are shown a video recording of an assembly or something special that the children have done. Parents receive a great deal of praise and encouragement for the work they do with their children in and out of school and most of them are wholeheartedly supportive of the values programme. Indeed, the school happily and frequently acknowledges its debt of gratitude to the many who come in as helpers with tasks such as hearing children read.

The few parents who are critical, according to Neil Hawkes, have the effect of the sand in an oyster shell that produces the pearl. Their criticisms are taken seriously and help the staff to define the policies more clearly: it sharpens the wits to have to meet objections. Some, for example, favour the idea of boys settling their playground disputes with their fists, which is not allowed at West Kidlington. When a mum comes in and says, 'I tell my boy if anyone gives him any trouble he should sort them out,' and the answer is, 'Hitting isn't allowed here,' her riposte might well be, 'How's he going to survive where we live, there's fights round our way every day?'

For the most part, however, parental involvement is conventional: discos, fund-raising events, fetes, educational trips and meetings with teachers about individual children's progress. There are ten kinds of meeting at West Kidlington, meetings between teachers and parents, parents and the head, the PTA, meetings with governors, meetings for curriculum considerations, meetings for reconsidering the values core, etc. These ten forums maintain communication and keep the balance between the needs of parents, teachers and children and the demands of the various regulatory bodies. Sometimes people feel there are too many meetings and sometimes they complain, but in fact the key to the whole thing running smoothly and harmoniously is the greatest possible exchange of information and understanding, in terms not only of quantity but also of quality. Staff meetings always focus on thinking about the practice and do not, in the headmaster's phrase, 'degenerate into information-giving sessions and diary sessions that go, "what are we going to do at the Christmas party?"'

This account of the first three years' evolution of the values programme at West Kidlington Primary School is simply a snapshot of work in progress at the point where the ethos is firmly in place. Everything is to be positive, excellence is to be praised, the children play a large part in decision-making and take exceptional responsibility for aspects of running the school. Behavioural demands made upon the children apply equally to the adults; there is flat management of administrative tasks, democratic decision-making and constant reassessment of ways of putting the values into every aspect of life. And having said all that, nothing is set in aspic, the whole enterprise continues to evolve.

THE KIDLINGTON BLUEPRINT

Some parents may find the positive values in use at West Kidlington suit them very well, others may prefer to choose their own value words. You could have twelve new ones every year. Work them out as a family: each choose a few. Or stick with these and add a couple more for a two-year cycle.

- A month is long enough for a child to absorb a good deal of meaning from the use of these positive concepts. Define the words carefully at the beginning, using stories and plays.

- With older children, you may sometimes refer to the Bible or other religious books that they can investigate for clues.

- A family conversation about what the words mean can be illuminating.

- With tiny children, the discussion must always be concrete, since they are too young for abstract thinking. As an example, there is the explanation of the word simplicity for the five- and six-year-olds in Year One. They were asked, 'What do you like best?' They answered perhaps predictably, a goodnight kiss from my Mum or Dad, a cuddle, a flower or a colour. The teacher said these were all *simple* things, not complicated, not costing money, the pretty and joyful things of every day.

- Above all, let conversation about value words be joyful, never oppressive!

- Let the children make cards or posters of the words and stick them somewhere noticeable. Let the words penetrate your consciousness as a reminder of an ideal, harmonious, achievable world.

- As grown-ups, these are among our tasks:

  – Praising excellence.

  – Sharing decision-making.

  – Abiding by the principles you lay down.

  – Forgiving and forgetting.

CHAPTER 4

Lessons

I NTEGRATED INTO EXISTING LESSONS THE POSITIVE VALUE WORD OF THE moment inevitably has greater or lesser relevance according to the subject being taught. West Kidlington is state-funded and must teach the nationally laid-down curriculum, with the correct number of hours devoted to all subjects. In Great Britain, the government says what must be taught in primary schools and to an extent when it must be taught, and maintains a testing system to measure progress. Naturally, the school follows the rules. It does very well in the national league tables of test results despite its location within an insalubrious area, with its share of children from disadvantaged households and 30 per cent having educational difficulties of one kind or another.

No time is included in the government allocation for teaching any subject that could come under the heading of values, or for the classroom examination of behaviour, hence the need to scatter the programme throughout the curriculum. The 20 per cent of the timetable over which schools can use their discretion has to include all extra activities such as visits to theatres or museums; even sport falls into this category. West Kidlington uses some of the tiny proportion of time that is left over in the prescribed school week for its dedicated values lessons, of which more later.

In fact, however, the time constraint actually strengthens the programme since it means that the work is subtly ever-present. The teachers believe that constant reiteration of the value words and observation of their practical results are needed for the children to see their full implications, and it is frequently noted that the children's own reference to the positive concepts strengthens their ability to resolve things that trouble them. The concepts are the foundation and the framework upon which the children can build their houses; therefore the teachers build the value words not only into the subject disciplines but also into all other school situations whether social or sporting. (This principle applies equally to their use at home.) The value words come into the rational subjects, science and maths, only in the course of tangential moral or behavioural discussions.

The Ofsted inspectors (a government appointed body) noted that skills required for the values work enhance all the academic efforts at West Kidlington. Their report marked the attitudes to learning in the school, 'very good,' said they contributed directly to the high standards of achievement, and remarked of the pupils: 'during lessons they listen attentively and respond quickly and positively to instructions from their teachers. They show commitment to their work, sustain concentration for long periods and respond increasingly well to challenging tasks.' By focusing constantly on positive concepts and ensuring practice in reflection, the programme was seen to create the climate and provide the means for serious, considered study.

Neil Hawkes, however, sees the purpose of the values work not as a simple task of skills creation but as nothing less than the creation of a community in which, 'we are all self-aware within the wider society.' If this high ambition is achieved, 'children are well-rounded and able to go to secondary school adaptable and flexible and motivated, and able to cope with the curriculum without being stressed.' The intention is to build sound, positive principles into the psyche and into its practical expression, strengthening the children to the point where, 'in later life when they come up against sticky situations, hopefully they won't just duck out.' In most schools, the emotional state of children is ignored until it results in tears or tantrums or disruptive behaviour. By contrast, West Kidlington aims to create a calm and happy environment for learning, believing that since the effect of the context upon the individual is perceived to be crucial, it is crucially important to get it right. As Karen Errington says, 'An unhappy child is not going to learn.'

Measuring the effect

An exercise on this question was undertaken by Linda Heppenstall, who asked her class to measure their current state of happiness on a scale of 0 to 10, with 0 signifying misery and 10 ecstasy. The first question was, 'How are you now?' and the second, 'How might what happens in the day affect you?' She put to them the idea that they could control what happened when people said x or y to them, whether they were reactive or whether they could listen and respond without emotional turmoil. 'Practise not being dependent on events that come along,' was the requirement. This is a fine demonstration of learning how not to react but developing the habit of thinking before making a response. It applies in conversation: the children pause before answering questions in a considered way.

Here is a summary of high quality, written by Kate, aged ten.

'To gain high quality at school.

Show respect for others.

Tell the truth.

Have patience.

Be kind and helpful to others.

Always try to do your best.

Care and show respect for your own and others' property.

Remember to say "please" and "thank you".

Apologise if you have done something wrong.

Be friendly and always smile (leave bad moods at the door).

Listen carefully when other people talk.

Raise your hand when you want to speak.

Work well with everyone in the class.

Be sensible – laugh at the right times.'

The practical expression of the positive concepts is seen during the rest of the school day. 'Children need the opportunity to know the difference between learning what it means in theory, and then making the leap into their own lives,' says Neil Hawkes. 'They need to see how creating positive thoughts leads to a happy existence. By making it part of the life of the school, it becomes part of how we live. We're moving into the parents' consciousness by putting the values into *Dolphin News*. If you were presenting this to an audience you'd explain there are four stages: telling, discussion, understanding and practising having the value.'

Before one of the school inspections, Neil Hawkes asked the teaching staff to observe the ways in which they were including Spiritual, Moral, Social and Cultural (SMSC) elements in their everyday teaching. The teachers came up with some illuminating observations, which showed that aspects of the work appear more or less everywhere. John Heppenstall specialises in Information Technology, not the most obviously spiritual subject, and gave this account:

Spiritual: As the children become more and more independent in the use of IT, they develop the quality of self-reliance.

Moral: Children working independently in IT require a developed sense of integrity and trustworthiness, so these qualities are encouraged.

Social: When using IT, children often work co-operatively.

Cultural: We can access information about other cultures by using CDs, e.g. Encarta, Ancient Lands. In the not too distant future we expect to be in direct contact with other cultures by joining the Internet.'

John Heppenstall says, 'Children are not simply empty vessels that can be filled up. The academic work is important – that's how schools are assessed – but we have to be concerned with the whole child. I believe you can only see effective teaching when everything is in place, when the children are happy and motivated, behaving themselves, and there's a positive relationship with the teacher. You see here very often classrooms when all those things are in place. The spiritual development of the child – the teaching of values – is one aspect of the picture and it has to come into the curriculum whether we like it or not. You need to have the children all working, but none of them frightened. They need to feel that what they're doing has a purpose! It's very complex.'

Physical education is another interesting discipline for consideration in the light of the values programme. Traditionally held to be the great socialiser and character-builder it still retains memories of some of the stirring slogans that propped it up in days gone by. Many people from either side of the public/private school divide can recall that, 'it matters not who won or lost, but how they played the game!' *Chiz, chiz*, as the great English public school commentator Nigel Molesworth used to say. He knew what the remark was worth: in fact, it mattered like crazy who won. It mattered to the house, and because it reflected badly not only on the physique but also on the moral fibre of the individual members of the losing team, it mattered greatly to everyone in that team. As for the winners, for them to pretend that winning didn't matter was simply nonsense: they were, to a greater or lesser level of modesty, glorious.

The vital activities of socialising and character building are, of course, perceived differently at West Kidlington School and it follows that their physical education outlook is different too. The words describing it sound similar but as always the emphasis is the crucial difference, and the difference is in the fine-tuning and in the assumptions behind it. PE teacher Sara Pack gave the following account on her SMSC report sheet for the school inspectors.

> '**Spiritual:** Developing the inner determination to succeed, do your best and have a sense of fair play.
>
> '**Moral:** When a game is completed children are encouraged to cheer each other and shake hands.
>
> '**Social:** Working as a team and showing respect for each other.
>
> '**Cultural:** Children in the rugby tournament took on the names of international sides.'

The difference is, as always, qualitative. When the children cheer each other and shake hands they really, genuinely mean it. On Sports Day you can't help but notice the enormous enthusiasm and gusto of the participants, who incidentally are not obliged to take part. Only those who genuinely wish to run the traditional 50 yards egg-and-spoon, obstacle or sack races do so. Sports children who trip over simply get up and carry on, or pick their egg up off the ground and put it back in the spoon and set off again, cheered even more enthusiastically by their classmates. At the end, the spectators applaud the winner but no one seems particularly bothered about victory or glory or even points.

However, on Junior Sports Day one of the mothers was heard fretting on the sidelines. 'I don't think they're competitive enough,' she said, but qualified it by observing that as her seven-year-old daughter's ambition was to become a vet she supposed competitiveness might not be so important in her life. It turned out that the woman's husband had recently been passed over for a promotion and she was feeling sensitive about the importance of competition and the unfairness of the commercial world. But had she a point? Not competitive enough?

'Not everyone can be winners,' says Neil Hawkes, 'not everyone even wants to be a winner. The emphasis on winning makes losers of 99 per cent of the field, most of whom actually don't care that much about winning anyway. That's the mistake the competitive society makes: not everyone wants to be a winner or a leader, most people just want to get on with doing whatever they're best at. We should validate that. Let those who want to be leaders and can do it, get on with it. Let those who just want to do what they do in the background, do that. We shouldn't make losers of the people who never wanted to come first.'

Parent–governor Andrew Jones agrees with this sentiment, he loved the whole event. 'I think this is wonderful,' he said. 'I want school Sports Day to be like this! There's so much goodwill, this is real sportsmanship as far as I'm concerned, fun, physical activity, everybody having a good time and doing their best. Who cares if you don't win?' Thus Sports Day can be seen as another demonstration of the ethos: great to win, great to take part, and all's well either way. In contrast to the traditional, theoretical assertion that it matters not who won or lost, this is the genuine article in practice.

Value words in literature: 1

The value words are used in the classroom with varying levels of intensity. They are simply brought as often as possible into the ordinary school day. Some lessons in arts subjects, however, are tailor-made for it. Here, Betty Brands' Year Sixes are examining Frances Hodgson Burnett's classic children's story, *The Secret Garden*. The children have read the book and are being asked to comment on the character of the heroine, Mary Lennox. The school inspectors' report says, 'Reading and speaking and listening are strengths of the school with attainment well above average. Pupils are enthusiastic about books and enjoy reading stories and poems at home and at school. They talk knowledgeably about books and can discuss favourite authors and characters.' Let's see.

Betty Brands' class have been asked for adjectives describing Mary Lennox. The teacher writes them on the board. She welcomes all the suggestions since they are all appropriate. They begin with *tyrannical*.

Betty Brands What does that mean?

Girl It's like my little brother, he has little tantrums.

The word tyrannical is associated with tantrums and other children mention them. Several of the class mention younger siblings with half-affectionate annoyance, and the word *little* is taken up and used more than once. More words are called for and in quick succession we get: *grumpy, stubborn, spoilt, sour, disagreeable, ugly attitude, unemotional* [meaning cold], *childish and shallow* – but none of the words is spoken pejoratively. The children seem to be dispassionate about Mary and often qualify a word by saying, 'that's because nobody bothers with her,' or 'you can see why.' You begin to sense their sympathy, which becomes overt later on.

For those who have forgotten the plot of *The Secret Garden* here it is: grumpy, stubborn, spoilt, sour, disagreeable Mary Lennox has been brought up in India mostly by her Ayah (servant). Her mother is remote and she has no friends. Her parents die suddenly and Mary is summoned back to England to live with her reclusive, depressive uncle on the bleak, inhospitable Yorkshire moors. However, the uncle is away travelling and Mary has to live more or less alone in part of his large house. Expecting service in the style of the Raj she is nonplussed to find herself treated in the brusque northern manner by some of the servants, and made to mind her manners. There is no one to talk to. She has never seen cold, grey skies and finds them depressing.

The tide begins to turn when she starts to dress in warm clothes and take herself out for walks. The fresh air and open countryside revive her health and spirits and she makes friends with a robin, a taciturn gardener, and finally Dickon, a country boy who can communicate with the moorland animals and always has one or two of them about his person. Mary's adventures out of doors take her ultimately to a key to the door of the secret garden, which is within walls and wholly overgrown. It has an extraordinarily powerful atmosphere. Mary feels at once much more at peace with herself and determines that with Dickon's help she will clear up the garden and make the flowers grow again. Meanwhile, she has met the invalid boy Colin who has been shut up in a bedroom in the west wing, tended by the servants and allowed – almost encouraged – to rot. He has a fiendish and hysterical temper. These two poor misfits strike up a friendship, Mary gets Colin in his wheelchair into the garden, all three children work together and Colin recovers as the garden begins to flourish. Finally, the children and Colin's father are united, with all their griefs and torments well on the way to total cure.

Betty Brands draws a circle around the adjectives and asks, 'Why do you think Mary is all these things?' The children put their hands up to speak and they answer in turn. 'No one loves her.' 'She hasn't any friends.' 'She's lonely.' 'No one wants her.' Their answers are written on the board.

'Is it really true that no one wants her?' asks Betty Brands. The children say that it has been true in the past, her mother seemed not to spend any time with her and her Ayah was sacked for being too nice, which made

Mary cry a lot, but that later in Yorkshire Colin and Dickon want her.

Betty Brands Why does Colin want her?

Children He's lonely. He's in bed all the time. He's bored.

Betty Brands Why does Dickon want her?

Girl He's only got animals to talk to. (This seems less plausible since Dickon has a large and comfortable family, but it is allowed to pass.)

Up to this point the values/literature lesson has shown how the values work has affected the pupils' general outlook. Now, the value words are named for directly personal application.

Betty Brands Shut your eyes and think of the values you've been taught, that make you be more like you are and less like Mary. Now open your eyes again, put your hands up and tell me some. Yes?

Boy Respect!

Betty Brands Yes, quite right. Who could have taught Mary respect?

Children Mrs Medlock [the housekeeper]. Her parents.

A boy says, 'If they wanted a child they should have shown her.' Betty Brands clarifies this and the boy confirms that he does indeed mean shown her how to behave. We can understand his concern, if Mary's parents wanted children they should have done the work of bringing them up. They have fallen down on their obligation.

Betty Brands That's right. They should have shown her. Who could show her now?

Girl Martha! Dickon!

Betty Brands Right. What else could be taught Mary that would help her, of the values you've been learning?

Boy Unity.

Betty Brands Good, how?

Girl If they gave her someone to play with.

Betty Brands How would that teach unity?

Boy Because you're working together.

Betty Brands points out that Mary has begun to learn a little unity, as is clear when she shows Colin how to do something, and instead of shouting at him she takes him through it slowly and quietly. The teacher asks for another value.

Boy Co-operation.

Betty Brands Keep going!

Girl When she was with her Ayah she just gave orders. Now she has to understand that people can say no.

Betty Brands Good, yes, what did she need to learn?

Boy Patience. She gets stroppy, she's never been taught how to wait for things.

Betty Brands How could we help her with her feelings, if she was here?'

Girl She could find out how to express them.

A boy volunteers that he has seen a programme on television about how men can't express their feelings. Betty Brands agrees that this is sometimes – though not always – true, then she moves the conversation back to the book and the qualities of patience and tolerance that would be needed in dealing with Mary and Colin if they are to get out of their social isolation. The children observe that Mary's trouble is that she can't tell anybody how she feels.

Betty Brands If you can't tell somebody how you feel, what'll happen?

Boy You'll get stroppy.

The class considers the proposition that when you can't express how you feel you get angry, and Betty Brands suggests that if that happens to them, it is possible to slow down, clear their head and have a reflective thought. Sit for ten minutes, she suggests, empty your mind, concentrate on your breathing.

Girl You can't!

Betty Brands I bet you can. You do it in the morning in assembly, don't you? If you try, I bet you can sit very quietly and clear your mind.

There's a slight rumble of disbelief but an important point has been made: you can take command of your mood. This is not at all the same as suppressing or hiding it. The cause of your mood can be talked through later if necessary but the strong emotion can be calmed down so that it does not disrupt your day. This is harmonious with the discipline of reflection that teaches the children to focus, concentrate and ultimately to command their thoughts. Thus the positive emphasis can be maintained and is not contingent on outside influences: the children become their own masters. The lesson continues.

Betty Brands Has Mary loved something or someone in her life?

Boy Her mum. Her Ayah.

Betty Brands Good, right, another value!

Girl Friendship! Appreciation!

Betty Brands Yes, Mary is *appreciating* the way Dickon talks, his knowledge, and his gift of his time, his loyalty to a friend. Think about these values and what you're missing if you haven't got some of them.

And that's the end of the lesson. It bears out what the school inspectors said: 'From an early age, pupils speak confidently and are able to express ideas. They are interested in what others have to say and are good listeners. Older pupils listen and respond to the ideas and feelings of others and are confident and articulate.'

How many primary aged children have the chance to consider in this depth the emotional condition of heroes and heroines of fiction, to sympathise with them even when they are behaving unsympathetically, to observe what is going on in their lives, to see all sides of complex questions? Children's natural sense of justice is encouraged by this means and not suppressed.

One more positive aspect of the positive values framework is that it seems to facilitate this sophisticated analysis. It is not just a useful tool for helping the children to behave well and be happy, it also provides a means for them to consider books and stories, other people's problems, a means by which they can experience empathy at the same time as sharpening their critical faculties. It appears to teach the capacity for a kind of objectivity, which is not just cold reason but sympathetic observation, a different kind of criticism, a positive kind.

Value words in literature: 2

Textual analysis is undertaken at all ages in slightly different ways. In the next example, John Heppenstall is coincidentally also teaching Year Sixes, but a different group from Betty Brands'. These children will go to secondary school next summer, so they are at the most sophisticated end of the West Kidlington cycle. Since the values programme has been in place for about three years this group came into it relatively late in their school lives. It is also a relatively new group to John Heppenstall, who is delighted as much by their self-discipline and the near-immaculate manner in which they arrive in the classroom and settle themselves as by the perspicacity of the observations they make on the book they have been reading.

'I've never seen children come into a room in such an orderly and good-humoured way, ready to work,' he says. 'It's nothing short of marvellous. The concentration's there already, you don't have to work for it.' The teachers frequently remark on this, their wonderment perhaps the more wonderful since it is their own everyday working environment that they find so consistently amazing. John Heppenstall's pleasure in his class's good behaviour is the more delightful as he has been teaching at the school for 20 years.

This class has read most of *Goodnight Mr Tom* by Michelle Magorian. The story is set in the 1930s and tells of William, a London child whose mother treats him exceptionally badly, who has no friends and is neglected to the point of malnourishment. During World War Two he is evacuated to the country. His renaissance begins, rather like Mary Lennox's, through the help of sympathetic people who make him feel like a human being for the first time. John Heppenstall has brought some of the values words, written on big pieces of coloured board, from the assembly hall. He turns them away from the class and asks the children to guess which ones he has that they might have detected in the book: an interesting exercise, even if only for the sake of recalling the concepts. When the children name the values that he has in his hands, he turns the boards round. They are: co-operation, friendship, helpfulness, happiness, honesty, quality and unity. All these will be needed says John Heppenstall, for the boy in the story to be at peace with the world and grow up strong and secure.

John Heppenstall How do you think you might feel if you were asked to take in a strange child, into your home, sharing all your things, for a month? Or even a week, or maybe a year? Answer honestly!

But he has no need to ask for honesty, all the children say at once that they wouldn't like it. There is no pretence, they are clear it would be an intrusion.

John Heppenstall What would be needed, apart from the values we've got here, if the adults in this boy's life are going to make a difference?

Girl Caring.

John Heppenstall Does anyone show caring?

Boy Mr Tom.

John Heppenstall How does he show it? Give me some examples.

A girl explains that William wets the bed and Mr Tom not only doesn't scold him about it but says he understands why it's happening. Mr Heppenstall reads a passage describing the businesslike and friendly way in which Mr Tom (clearly in the market for a halo) changes wet sheets.

John Heppenstall How else does Mr Tom show caring?

Boy Teaches him to read.

John Heppenstall All right. (He shuffles his boards ready to be displayed one by one.) Let's look at the word *care*. What do people do for this child that shows they care for him?

Girl Look after him. Feed him. Clothe him.

John Heppenstall Good! Excellent! Next one, *respect!* How's that shown? You see I always want evidence, I don't just want the word, I want you to say how you know that something is so.

Children Not hitting him. Not shouting at him.

The negatives in this answer probably say more about the earlier treatment of the book's hero than they do about the understanding of the children, since the early chapters of *Goodnight Mr Tom* are taken up with descriptions of maltreatment, which have bitten deep.

John Heppenstall OK, now *thoughtfulness!*

Girl William's not used to it, he's surprised when people do things for him. When Mr Tom gives a party for his birthday he doesn't know what to do.

John Heppenstall Is he pleased about the party?

Boy He's never had one before, he doesn't know it's for him.

John Heppenstall Well, that's quite a thought, isn't it! You all have cards and presents and cake on your birthdays, so do I. Fancy never having had a birthday present! Let's look at another word. here it is!

John Heppenstall pulls *happiness* from the pile. The children continue on the birthday theme, mentioning that William shows surprise when there is love that appears to be intended for him. He cannot immediately understand that it could be so and experiences the beginnings of happiness. The class acknowledges that William has not known what it is to be happy. Next word.

John Heppenstall Honesty?

Girl People treat him right. His mother used to tell lies to him but Mr Tom doesn't.

John Heppenstall Friendship … The whole book is about this, isn't it? About William finding friendship and Mr Tom making a difference to his life. What do you think is going to happen in this book?

Boy He goes back to his mum, he doesn't want to.

John Heppenstall That's right, he doesn't want to. Now there's a terrible idea, not wanting to go back to your mum! But maybe now he's grown stronger and he knows people love him, Mr Tom and some of the other people in the village love him, he'll be able to help his mum with whatever has gone wrong in her life that's made her so unhappy. Do you think?

The children don't seem convinced and John Heppenstall moves on. 'Next one, *trust.*' he starts the ball rolling. 'William's finding out what it means,' he suggests.

Girl If children don't have anyone to trust they're miserable. He can't ask anyone to help him, if he doesn't trust them.

John Heppenstall Good! Smashing!

There are two boards to go. The first says *responsibility*, which the teacher explains is what Mr Tom has taken for William. He has seen where the trouble is and made it his business to put it right. The last word up is *tolerance*. A pupil says this means, 'you put up with it,' which seems fair enough. Mr Tom has put up with a great deal in his mission for William's renaissance. The class is nearly over and John Heppenstall says he's going to ask just one more question. He collects up the word boards and the children cluster round him, clutching their books and pencil cases, poised to move off for the next activity.

John Heppenstall You won't know the answer to this so don't worry. I'm just asking out of idle curiosity, really. There's been some talk about the Prime Minister at the time of this story. Who was the Prime Minister in the Second World War?

Boy At the beginning of the book it would have been Chamberlain. Later on it was Winston Churchill.

John Heppenstall Good heavens! How do you know that?

Boy I was reading it in Encarta.

The children collect the rest of their things and go, the teacher answering their questions or reminding them of things as they leave, the customary departure of children from a classroom.

'It's amazing what they pick up by themselves,' says John Heppenstall when the room is empty. 'Encarta! I thought one or two of them might get Churchill, but Chamberlain's going a bit, isn't it!' He is pleased with this, as he is with the insights into *Goodnight Mr Tom*. 'They can really relate the values to what they're learning,' he says, 'they tie it all together straight away. The whole thing ties in, the whole thing relates so well.'

Value words during an art class

It was much harder to see how values might tie in to Marion Trigg's Year Six art class. Surely drawing is a value-free activity? Was she going to guarantee a discussion of the current word, and if so, on what possible grounds? She began by taking the register, which is done almost ceremoniously, so it takes a little while and leaves time for examining the children's fine dragon model high on the wall and the classroom rules over the whiteboard. Every class determines its own rules and displays them. Marion Trigg's pupils have settled on:

- I am not going to disturb others when they are working.
- I am going to move around the classroom carefully, thinking about others.
- I am not going to interrupt.
- I will think of others not just myself.

The democratic agreement on the classroom rules strengthens them greatly. The children have talked through how they will try to behave for the term and reached consensus on it. They can see that the guidelines if adhered to will benefit the total effort and themselves. This technique is not exclusive to West Kidlington, many schools do it, but in fact good behaviour is something all visitors comment on and marvel at. A temporary teacher who usually teaches in a secondary school said of the values work, 'I think the children here take more care and trouble with ordinary tasks such as moving about the room because they are going about their day within a framework that they understand.'

On the whiteboard is pinned a reproduction of Albrecht Dürer's *Praying Hands*. When registration is finished and after a couple of minutes spent praising and thanking members of the class who looked after a disabled child in the playground earlier in the day, Marion Trigg moves to the contemplation of hands.

Marion Trigg What do we use hands for?

Children Touch. Draw. Write. Pick things up. Pray.

They begin to consider gesture, drama, action and mood. Suddenly, Marion Trigg glances sideways and points at a child.

Marion Trigg What does that gesture tell us?

Girl You're cross.

Marion Trigg If I point like that it might be that I've seen someone not paying attention, I might want to bring him or her back to concentrating on the class.

The teacher continues with this idea, shaking her finger at another child. The action is not threatening since everyone knows it is a demonstration and she smiles as she does it.

Marion Trigg What might I be saying if I do this gesture?

Boy Telling someone off.

A pupil volunteers that her mother has learned sign language so that she can look after a deaf child and a couple of the children begin to practise what looks like authentic signing. Throughout the lesson Marion Trigg has been mentioning the word concentration, and now she asks the children to look at the drawing of the hands, which is pinned to the white board.

Marion Trigg What are these hands doing?

Girl Praying.

Marion Trigg It seems as though when you're praying, you generally use your hands. You might not put them together like this, you might fold them in your lap, or hold them up like this (she demonstrates the raised palms position associated with Islam), but you're likely to use them. Why do you think that is?

Boy Helps you concentrate.

Marion Trigg That's right. And that's what you need when you're praying, or meditating, you need to keep your mind clear and focused. What else can hands show? What do you do if somebody's upset?

Girl Put your arm round them.

Marion Trigg That's right, put your arm round them, or hold their hand, or stroke them, these are all things your hands do to express emotion. So what are you expressing with your hands?

Children Kindness. Caring.

Marion Trigg Yes.

Next there is talk of drawing technique, shading, using the edge of the pencil, of the importance of careful observation and working slowly, of cupping the left hand slightly (for right-handed pupils) so as to see the movement. Then they match the right hand to the left to create the picture of the hands together.

'Do you remember when you were Year Twos, you would have just taken a strong black pencil and drawn round your fingers?' asks Marion Trigg. One or two of the children smile indulgently at their early simplicity. Once upon a time, their drawings were so primitive! 'I don't want that sort of drawing now,' continues the teacher. 'What I'm looking for is real observation, proper shading, a real impression of movement, of what the hands are doing. You need to work slowly for this one.'

The children are released from their places, there's a scuffle for paper, they settle at their tables, and straight away there follows an almost supernatural silence. What seems to have happened is that the conversation about the hands, the drawing technique and concentration, have worked a near-magical trick and the children are entirely engrossed in the difficult task of observing and sketching.

'Last year I took the hands theme into the values lesson,' explains Marion Trigg, referring to one of the specialised discussions. 'We were talking about prayers, and noticing movement. We got some good work from that. It's amazing how interested they are in this one! After half term I'm doing Christianity and I shall put their drawings of praying hands on the wall.'

But hands as symbolic of values?

'The point is that the talk we've had about this piece of work had a lot of values content,' says Marion Trigg. She thinks for a while. 'All we're doing in a class like this is backing up what parents would do. I just want to back up the fundamental things all parents would want to teach at home: kindness, consideration, caring. Other schools find it difficult to fit it into the curriculum; we do it throughout the subjects, that's all. We're all continuing the same values work, whatever the subject. It's all the same thing in different ways.' In fact, the gentle but frequent calls for concentration echo the school discipline of reflection that is so close to meditation. The hands and the subject matter tell their own tale.

Here once again are two of the strengths of the values programme: it runs throughout, and it is consistent. The fact that the teachers are all singing from the same hymn sheet makes school life safe and supportive for the children and the children respond positively to it. Marion Trigg was on playground duty after the drawing class and came back into her classroom saying that two of the pupils had continued the conversation with her in the break time; they were particularly interested in sign language, in the ability of hands to express particular words.

The artwork that resulted from this exercise was fine and various. Some drawings showed excellent draughtsmanship, some were simple. As had been promised, after half term the pictures were displayed neatly on a board. Interspersed among them were the computer-printed words: caring, peace, friendship, thoughtfulness, thankfulness, which had been emphasised during the discussion. One pupil had simply drawn around their fingers and written alliterative lists of manual actions down each of them: 'spilling, squashing,' started off the little finger, then came 'picking, pushing,' 'clapping, clutching,' 'locking, learning,' and on the thumb, verbs beginning with t, starting with 'touching, talking'. In large capitals across the palm was the legend: I LOVE MY HANDS.

Neil Hawkes thinks that because values are not in the consciousness, too many adults have abdicated responsibility for teaching them and have thus left a vacuum to be filled by television, by negative, materialistic messages from various sources. The novelty at West Kidlington is the use of the positive throughout all the academic exercises, the insistence on constructiveness even within the formal processes of deconstruction. This creates a state of mind that is capable of much greater objectivity. Here, schoolwork, and the integrated effort towards harmonising timetable, pupil, teacher and school is seen to be working. If personal improvement is also perceived to be the development of the balanced, contemplative child who can assess situations and people from a position of security and with a degree of objectivity, well, what a bonus that would be! Then there would be the achievement of the objective, which could perhaps be said to be the happy, hard-working child, living and learning within a harmonious community. It would be unfair to claim that West Kidlington achieved this ideal with all of its pupils all of the time, but it is fair to say that it does so for many of them for much of the time, and that in itself is remarkable.

Within the small amount of discretion allowed in the prescribed timetable, some time is taken every week at West Kidlington for each year group to consider the current value with its class teacher and to chew over moral dilemmas. During these lessons the children look at how they might have done things differently – or perhaps if what they did in a situation was after all in keeping with the concept and their conscience. This exercise in self-awareness, in the observation of each child's actions and their impact on the wider community, is possibly unique. It is undertaken under the leadership of the class teacher who is as far as possible impartial, although clearly even apparently bland observations made without vocal emphasis such as Linda Heppenstall's, 'but then nobody could play football, could they?' (see Chapter Three) carry some bias.

Value words during a circle time conversation

Here, Shirley Ball's Year Twos have returned to their classroom from a lunch hour that was too wet for them to play outside. They are feeling cooped up, nevertheless they must sit quietly and have their conversation, a formal task, which places quite a demand on them. First of all they sing the register. Shirley Ball sings, 'Jasmine, are you here?' Jasmine sings back, 'Yes, Shirley Ball, I am here!' – and so on. The children have been told there is a visitor and are, as always, well-mannered, not turning round to stare or whisper. The most they will do is glance across and smile at a stranger. This again is in contrast with what you find in many other schools.

Shirley Ball's class opened with some memories of the Christmas value word, which was *happiness*, and moved to the January word, which is *hope*. Shirley Ball combined the two. 'My hope at Christmas was that everybody would have a happy time,' she said. 'I wondered about an old man down the lane who lives alone but was ill in hospital.'

A little girl remarked that her family knows someone who lives alone. 'We gave her a box of food,' she said. A boy says an old lady in his village called for help on Christmas Day and they got her a doctor. Shirley Ball started on a box of objects she had prepared as conversation pieces for the topic. 'In my box I've got things to show you. I'm going to ask you what you think I was hoping for at the times when I was using the objects.' The first object was a black and white picture: an ultrasound scan of her daughter.

Shirley Ball When I saw that picture, what do you think I was hoping for?

Girl A girl?

Shirley Ball No, it didn't matter.

Boy A baby!

Shirley Ball Yes, I wished for a healthy baby, and that it would go very well.

A medal came out of the box. It belonged to Mr Ball's grandfather, who fought in the Second World War. He sent it home to his wife, who kept it close to her.

Shirley Ball What was she hoping for?

Girl That he wouldn't be hurt.

There were many more objects and photographs, many more comments; the children putting up their hands to speak and on the few occasions of children interrupting, being gently asked to wait for one another. Then the teacher summed up the conversation, which had been concerned with the hopes of young and old people. Lastly there was a picture of a little Indian girl. The children said she looked poor, lonely and sad. Why? They thought she might not have enough food or water. A boy said the picture made it look as though the girl's parents didn't take enough care of her. Shirley Ball explained that this eight-year-old Indian girl supported her family, and her life was hard.

Shirley Ball What might she hope for, do you think?

Boy Help.

Girl Something to eat.

The class generally concentrated well on this exercise despite the fact that they hadn't got out at lunchtime, which is perhaps especially troublesome for such a young group. There were two or three exits for the toilet, the teacher moved one or two children to sit close to her, but overall attention was held for nearly three-quarters of an hour, a very long time for Year Twos. The last task was to go round the circle and for the children to say what they hoped for in the world.

Lee I hope that everybody has a lovely home.

Jessica I hope all children have food.

Francesca I hope children get what they ask for.

Yasmin I hope all children are OK, I hope they're safe.

Fava I hope everybody stops fighting.

William I hope everybody takes care of everybody.

'Yes,' interjected Shirley Ball, 'We're here, we imagine we're all brothers and sisters at school, but it's not like that everywhere is it? Let's have some more hopes. What would you like people to be?'

Andrew Healthy.

Lewis Kind.

Kay Happy.

Ellis Everybody shares.

Robin There isn't a Third World War.

Izzy Everybody has money, doesn't have to be poor.

Tracy I hope in America they'll stop killing everybody because everybody's got guns.

Thomas Everybody is kind.

Matthew Mums and dads look after sisters and brothers.

Last of all it was Tao's turn. He is autistic but he takes part in some of the general lessons with his full-time care assistant. Tao smiled a big smile before making his contribution. '*I love everybody!*' he said.

'Well done, I think you've given good thoughts today!' said Shirley Ball, dispersing them to other tasks. She was pleased with the class.

'It worked pretty well,' she said. 'Something like *hope* is very abstract, I thought by bringing in something of my own, it would start the subject off. I was hoping for an understanding of someone else's life, what the other person might hope from it, and I think to an extent I got it.' The social dynamics of the class were noted. 'One of the most important things about a situation like this one is that the little ones learn that everyone's view is important. They must give each other time to answer. Then again, if they're off the point, you mustn't let them feel not valued. You have to bring the subject back without making them feel their opinion wasn't worth anything … Working in groups, co-operating, is still new. Who's on target, who finds it difficult – everything has got to be kept under constant review.'

The progress of the subject matter had been, as so often, from the personal to the general. What happened in the Christmas holidays, how the neighbours fared, what were the hopes of the children for themselves and for the world: the conversations are directed from the smaller to the larger focus. 'Who am I and what is my place in the world?' are constant questions, as is, 'How do my actions affect the community in which I find myself?' Shirley Ball believes this is invaluable. 'Every day we talk about how we treat each other, how we treat the classroom. It's a constant concern that we must live and work together harmoniously. I have to explain this to parents, that how we are individually and as a group is so important.'

A moment on this point. Political systems that concentrate heavily either on the success of the individual or on the over-riding importance of the national community miss this very problem, the problem of duality and balance. The question is simply that we live both as individuals and as parts of groups, that we are both singular and plural, that we must make our own way and yet support and be supported by our social grouping.

On top of the hillside stands a group of trees. Each must make its own roots and draw strength from the ground. Each must absorb light and rain and make leaves and shed them and make new ones again. But they stand in this exposed place together and if a gale comes, their combined strength will mean that they are not blown down. They stand as individuals and at the same time their existence as a group protects them. The difficulty of comprehending these simultaneous tasks has not always been resolved in schools, either.

THE KIDLINGTON BLUEPRINT

Some situations lend themselves spectacularly well to investigation and for developing a positive outlook. In others, the use of the positive value words is incidental. Constantly keep the word of the moment in view, taking the level of its understanding much deeper than simply the intellectual.

If as a family you are considering, say, *truthfulness*, and a conversation arises about someone in the news who has been caught lying, you could turn it into an investigation of conscience. The shades of black and white, whether promises must be kept to the letter, how far definitions can be shifted to suit occasions, provides a big subject. All children are concerned about truthfulness and they soon notice when adults' behaviour doesn't match their words. 'Walk your talk!' might have been invented by the young.

The value words have great potential for investigation. Keep in mind your family word and bring it into the conversation sometimes. In this way the concepts are absorbed into the subconscious and become the structure with which the children assess situations and behaviour and decide on their own course of action.

Some of the school lessons focus on ethics questions that concern the children. In others, such as the examinations of literature, the positive concepts are used as tools (see Appendix). They are invaluable in resolving everyday incidents. They make a safe framework not only for children but also for adults – how often the teachers and parents of the West Kidlington pupils say they find them helpful too!

We all have much to learn. Children love it when adults can own up to being confused sometimes too. Great harmony can come from the simple exercise of adults joining in.

CHAPTER 5

Assembly

A T West Kidlington School the Quiet Revolution takes place in many different ways and among the most obvious and powerful is the daily meeting, or assembly. In many schools the obligation to hold assemblies is seen as a chore and behind the legal requirement to hold some form of collective Act of Worship every day has been fermenting a great deal of dissent. Indeed, many schools have more or less abandoned them altogether. However, at West Kidlington they take the school or class assembly very seriously and hold one every day, all slightly different but all serving a positive purpose and contributing to the cohesive harmony that makes the school so unusual. The staff believe the point of the assemblies is to affirm the school's identity and aspirations. This is at the heart of all the morning meetings, whatever form they take.

A great deal of effort goes into the planning and presentation of what look like simple meetings to make sure that the precise atmosphere of alert stillness is created in the hall, the correct conditions for calm concentration, the exact balance of content. As with all the West Kidlington school activities the continuity of behaviour is exemplified by the teachers for the children. In many school assemblies you see teachers talking while children are expected to be silent, this is not so at West Kidlington and demonstrates one of its great, essential strengths – the personal commitment of all the adults in the school to proper behaviour. It follows that as much as there must be no teachers talking, there must be no teachers arriving late, since what is demanded of the children is also demanded of the adults. For the children, the very manner of walking into the assembly hall is critical: nudging and giggling and whispering are not seen.

Sue Booys is a Church of England vicar and a parent of a West Kidlington pupil, and she contributes to some of the assemblies. She says, 'the attention to detail matters very much. It matters that, for example, the head teacher is always in assembly before it starts – in many places a busy head would consider that a waste of time.'

Indeed, whoever is taking the assembly is always sitting in the hall before the children begin to file in silently. The children are accompanied by their class teachers and they wait for their signal to sit down, then they seat themselves cross-legged in rows. An autistic boy is brought in by his full-time care assistant, who helps him to sit and then seats herself behind him in case she is needed.

The near ceremonial nature of the beginning sets the tone and marks out the boundaries. It looks old-fashioned but in fact it is not, and instead of feeling restrictive, it actively creates security. There are no sulky or miserable faces. Though the children walk in silence they are not oppressed, they are already imbibing the spirit of the event, and the harmony of the community is beginning to assert itself. Their faces are bright, they are ready to join in the meeting, they are focused upon it – and by extension, focused upon the school and the day to come.

West Kidlington assemblies are carefully designed. The process begins with the staff brainstorming of the central idea. The source materials are drawn from the major world faiths with Christianity paramount since it is the main religion of the British Isles, although reference is also made to Buddhist, Hindu and Islam traditions. The foundation for all of the assemblies are the elements of peace, harmony and positive thoughts. Reverend Sue Booys says, 'I would think of West Kidlington as a multifaith school, and as a faith-full school. They all believe that life has a spiritual dimension that is important. For me, that dimension is Christianity, but the first point is spirit.' She is full of praise for the atmosphere. 'From the children's point of view, calmness brings an expectation. The sense of value placed on other people encourages them to value themselves and to realise that the reflection is for themselves. When I do an assembly I know I shall get a receptive audience, children with whom I can talk easily, children who are receptive to prayer. You don't have to work at a sense of what you're doing being worthwhile, which makes it a much more valuable experience for me as well as them.' The multifaith aspect is endorsed by Maz Yaqooeb, a Muslim whose son is at West Kidlington School. She says her boy is taking weekly Urdu lessons at the local mosque and she is more than happy that all the spiritual work in the school is harmonious with his other studies.

Monday

On the first day of the week Neil Hawkes always takes the assembly. The month's theme word is introduced. (This is in addition to the week's word, which is in the spirit of the government's prescribed acts of worship for schools throughout the country.) Year Three teacher Louise Conroy expresses the staff-room consensus when she says the Monday assembly is critically important. 'It's essential for the staff as well as the children. You have to bring your attention back to school. You need to focus on school and duty and the children, and the Monday assembly pulls all that together. I enjoy it, but I need it too. I think it serves more purposes than you can really define.' In a community that works in groups as intensely as a school does, the restoration of purposeful concentration to each individual participant will be effective upon the whole. Hence the full-strength assembly on Monday, the head sitting quietly in the room, the Junior school in attendance.

In the gymnasium/assembly hall, a reflective atmosphere has been created with lighting and music. The PTA bought the stereo system, there are microphones so that the children's voices can be amplified if necessary; coloured spotlights create pools of light which concentrate attention on the centre of activity, a candle burns at the front of the hall and the assembling children can focus upon it. Light comes in through huge skylights and from the side corridor. The room is plain, neither fussily decorated nor wholly blank. Pleasant, calming music plays on a tape. Neil Hawkes sits in the state of stillness that he wishes the children to have, silently observant, still but not passive, attentive to the hall but concentrated within himself. He is also making eye contact with individual children in order to make a personal connection with them. When everyone is in place, he stands up and starts the assembly.

Neil Hawkes Welcome! I hope you used the weekend to do things … I did a lot of things, lots of them were good fun, some were relaxing and some were chores, and this morning I was out in the garden early, looking at my pond, which is a favourite place in my garden. I saw it first with raindrops falling on it, they were bouncing on the surface, then when the rain stopped I saw it when it was quite still. Then a dragonfly landed on it and that brought a surface change, little ripples moved outwards from where this very beautiful insect had been. The surface of a pond is like our thoughts: sometimes jangly, sometimes peaceful. We

need to make our minds relaxed but alert, so we can deal with
our problems without upsetting ourselves.

Thus the week begins, with a greeting to everyone, the hope that they had
a pleasant weekend, a brief reference to the activities within it, a visual story
with a harmonising purpose. The transition between home and school,
work and play is being set in motion. Next a song is announced, the positive,
life affirming sort, vaguely but not always overtly religious. The words are
projected on to the wall by an overhead projector operated by two of the
children and the tune is played on the piano by a member of staff or it may
be on the tape recorder. Staff and children join in more or less lustily. Many
of them know the words by heart since they practise the songs in whole
school choir practice every Wednesday. To start the week when they were
concentrating on global awareness of the need for countries to co-operate,
for example, they sang *World in Union*. Alternatively, there might be *The sun
has got his hat on!* or *The wise man built his house upon the rocks*. A particular
favourite with the younger children goes, *If I were* … this or that animal,
a butterfly perhaps, or a busy, busy bee, and each verse has the rousing,
exuberant chorus 'but I just thank you Lord for making *me!*'

Next there is likely to be a story, often practical and homespun, possibly
describing something ordinary that happened over the weekend, possibly
a simple story from the Bible or other sacred text. The story gives rise to contemplative thought. It will link into the theme and lead to another more
general thought, there may be a moment of silence focusing upon the
current word, and then there is whole assembly reflection. All this applies
to the very young children too. (In assemblies for the younger pupils the
story always involves them in movement – stepping out to play a part, 'who
would like to come out and play Joseph's wife?' or joining hands, or looking
in a certain direction – and there is always a demand for concentration and
understanding.) The final request is for reflection. Here is the one that was
used on 17 June.

Neil Hawkes This morning in a moment of silence let us sit very
still, close our eyes and feel relaxed. On the screen of your mind,
see yourself in your classroom, working hard at an activity, co-
operating with others. Feel good about this work. Now think
about our month's value – the value of *trust* – and think about
someone you really trust. How do we become trustworthy, so
others will trust us? What qualities do we need to develop?

Patience, tact, friendliness, co-operation, honesty, may be some of
the qualities. Choose one to think about during the day ... Now
open your eyes again.

The practice of reflection is at least as rare in schools as it is in the larger
world. Here it is led, focused; it is the beginning of the school day, the beginning of the school week. It brings the children back to focus upon the
positive aspects of themselves that they can value and build on. In a world
that has taken to harping on about low self-esteem it is almost immeasur-
ably useful to bring each child back to their central value, to the parts of
themselves of which they can feel most proud. Educationalists who are concerned about a trend towards short-term concentration may look with
wonder upon the children of West Kidlington School who can sustain a
school assembly of 20–25 minutes without talking or giggling. They can
also focus on it, maintain the idea, and finally remain for several minutes
in silent contemplation of a positive concept (what previous generations
might have called a virtue).

They do sustain it, the meeting is closed with a prayer, the tape goes
back on and the orderly processions begin again, leaving in the same lines
in which they arrived. There is total calm. It takes several minutes for the
children to leave the hall and during that time Neil Hawkes sits at the front,
not moving, not talking, but contemplative, and once again takes the opportunity of making eye contact with individual children. The teachers who
brought their rows of children into the room signal to the children to rise
in the order they came in, and in that order they leave. Those who are
waiting to go, wait in silence.

The effect of this Monday assembly, like all the Monday assemblies,
has been to bring the school back together again, to re-focus upon the week
in view, on its objectives and the tools that will be used to achieve them.
What is being demonstrated is a remarkable synthesis of the reiteration of
the value of each child and their individual thoughts and abilities, reiteration of the importance of those elements to the community, reiteration of
the secure place of each child within the school. Finally, at a subtle but powerful level, it provides a reminder to each child and adult in the assembly
hall of the importance of the school community itself. Indeed, a very complex web of ideas, observations and intentions has been woven. The children
have been invited to consider their inner capabilities, their positive worth,
their place in the community and their purpose for the week, and to do it
from the touchstone of that month's positive and unifying concept. They

have been invited and they have answered the invitation in the affirmative, so that now they are focused, positive, calm and ready to start.

This daily event is actively enjoyed by the pupils who say they like it while they are at West Kidlington School and miss it when they leave. Such enjoyment contrasts with a widespread distaste among the general public for assemblies or meetings. It is one that somehow goes along with a wringing of hands over the loss of the extended family, the breakdown of the nuclear family and the dissipation of many of the traditional frameworks for providing individual security and defining social behaviour. This wringing of hands makes no connection between the two.

Meanwhile the phenomenon of social fragmentation, famously expressed as 'there's no such thing as society', manifests not only as personal distress for very many people but also as confusion about where we belong and who are our neighbours. Nowadays we are not used to assembling or behaving as groups, indeed we rather despise it, so great has been the emphasis on the individual and on success with a thrilling, competitive edge. And yet at the same time we desperately miss our context: the village, the sense of belonging to a community, the long-established support networks.

Many social mechanisms such as church-going or membership of local societies are declining and the perception of cause and effect is clear: without a core, whether of family, industry, activity, belief system or all of them, society and social life are confused and fragmented. However a marvellous opportunity for re-creating at least some part of it exists in every school, and it is school assembly.

If you want to weld a group of people together for any purpose at all, then the notions of common purpose and common worth can be extremely useful. How much more powerful it is if each member of the community has been invited to find the purpose and worth within him or herself, and to see it as part of the whole. These are not new ideas. It is the manner of presenting them and the continuity of this particular school community that are new, and the emphasis on individual responsibility that applies right down to the five-year-olds at West Kidlington is nothing short of extraordinary. For many years attempts to weld schools together have been based upon edicts from above, made with admonishments and threats and backed by systems of punishment. At West Kidlington, the school community starts from the individual child and the value of each one, and allows them to see their part in their own world. 'If I do this, how will it affect me – and how will it affect the others?' is the question they are constantly taught how to ask, gently but definitely, and they understand that their responsibility is to themselves and to the total effort at the same time. This understanding is begun in assembly.

The teachers find the spiritual exercises invaluable too. When they take the assemblies they must work within government guidelines and simultaneously maintain the ethical position of the school, and they generally end up holding a meeting that looks a lot like the head teacher's. They do this with great aplomb and some differences of style and they say that it teaches them a great deal and touches them inwardly also. Neil Hawkes's notes for guidance of the staff who wish to take assemblies make some important observations. They include these:

'Our assemblies, which include our Acts of Worship [the legal obligation], are an important feature of our school's life. They act as one of the main ways by which we create our positive reflective ethos and promote our values-based education. I am grateful to all colleagues who make a positive contribution to them. In fact, all colleagues make a tremendous contribution through their presence and active participation. Pupils are very aware that all staff, by their positive attitude, involve themselves in assemblies, acting as role models for the pupils to emulate.

'Assemblies should contain times of quiet reflection, which enable pupils to develop the deepest values and aspirations of the human spirit (e.g. love, peace, wonder, imagination, sensitivity and integrity).

'Silent reflection is a key element in our Assemblies. It is especially important to remind pupils about expected behaviour when coming to and returning from the Hall across the playground.'

Thus, the manner of the assembly is also understood to be a critical part of it and a key factor in its total impact.

Of the school and its ethos the Reverend Sue Booys says, 'the most important thing is wholeness. A whole community. This is not a place that is only devoted to teaching children *things*. The function of the school is that the children learn their academic stuff more effectively because they learn in a valued, structured environment. The quality of learning is better, and life skills and values are absorbed in ways they are in few other schools. No detail about people, individuals, or the conduct of the school, is considered unimportant. There's a clear sense of vision.'

Tuesday

The Juniors have the assembly hall and the younger children go to similar assemblies in their own classrooms. This Junior assembly is taken by a class teacher and today it is Karen Errington's turn. After the children have filed in she announces the song and when they sing *Hushabye mountain* rather too quietly she asks them for a little more volume and gets it.

It is nearly the end of the summer term so when the teacher asks the children to close their eyes for a moment and then says, 'If you were packing a suitcase …', some minds dart to the holidays, but the sentence continues rather unexpectedly '… for a baby,' and goes on with a big question, 'what would you put in for the whole of its life on earth?' Karen Errington asks the children to open their eyes and give their suggestions: 'toys', 'teddy', 'loving care', 'clothes', 'good health', 'money', 'education', 'friends'. Next, there's a Bible story about a farmer who had too much grain and began to build a bigger barn to store it in rather than give the surplus away, but died in the night before he could enjoy the riches the extra grain would bring him. Foolish farmer!

Karen Errington How do you feel when you give a present?

Children I like the expression on their face. Makes me feel warm.
You can feel a bit shy.

The general view is that giving a present makes you feel very good. The assembly continues and after about quarter of an hour there is some minor shuffling, but still no talking. Three children read short poems they have written; then the teacher takes the meeting back into her own hands. The final message is this: 'Close your eyes and think about the richness in your life, the things you can't buy: a special memory, a hug from someone special, chatting with someone special, knowing you are loved. Just one special thing that you really like.' Silence. Music. It's over. Then the orderly, silent departure.

Karen Errington is delighted and a little surprised by the children's responses to the question of packing the baby's suitcase. 'I'm pleased with that,' she says, 'I'd expected more material things and I thought I would have to lead them around to the more abstract ones, like love and health and friends. I think it shows they've taken in a lot this term. Hope so!' She is leaving to take up a deputy headship and says she is glad that she has taken the opportunity the school has afforded her of taking her own assemblies. 'It's important while we're here that we experience everything,' she says. 'The assemblies in particular have been useful. You learn a lot from watching other people's. The head always models the value for the week – that's been brilliant, that quality. You can watch it and then do it in your own way. I've been in schools where assembly would just be a painful experience of crowd control. Here, they're much more focused. Using reflection asks the children to bring their own experiences, and draw from them. Here, with all of us there's a continuity, a harmony of presentation.'

Miss Errington is enthusiastic about the idea of taking the values education emphasis into the next school, indeed she says that at her job interview she made it a condition of taking up the post. 'I think it gives the children space and opportunity to think about their behaviour and others' behaviour, space to air their views. I've seen some marvellous assemblies while I've been here, and I can tell you that before I came I'd worked in several schools – four or five if you include my teaching practices – and I'd never walked into an assembly where all the children are silent and focused. The reason for it is that they've been trained since Infants. On the first day the teachers talk about the experience to the Infants, and the expectations, that assembly shouldn't be a passive arrangement. The children are reminded to move quietly around the school and they're shown how to line up. They know what's expected and they just do it, it's amazing. When I got here I couldn't believe it. A lot of people comment on it.'

The content of the assemblies has also made a great impression. 'We did an assembly last term on understanding,' she says, 'on the need to understand. The children were asked about understanding and they said we all needed to understand – why some of them can't read, or swim, things like that – then it moved into bigger things, why some of the children's parents couldn't get on. A boy whose parents' marriage was breaking up said he wanted the subject talked about, but that he himself couldn't talk about it because it would make him cry. I can't imagine anywhere else where that would have been possible, this is the most extraordinarily supportive place. It's the whole child we're concerned with – literacy, numeracy, heart and soul. The thing is, an unhappy child is not going to learn.'

Here is another powerful element: the children are so sensitive to one another's needs that they feel secure in introducing to the school assembly subjects of great emotional distress. Apparently the children who talked about the marriage breakdown acknowledged that it must be terrible for the boy but suggested that if his parents would be happier living separately, and the boy would be able to see them being happier, it might not be so bad after all. Then they offered him their sympathy. This is very grown-up stuff indeed and is entirely in keeping with the activities in the rest of the school. Teachers say the values work gives clarity of thought and it appears on this showing that it gives the children the clarity to think through even domestic catastrophe. It also enables them to put themselves in the position of their schoolmates, and to understand and share their troubles. And it all starts in assembly.

Karen Errington says, 'The whole-school ethos, the values work, it all genuinely empowers. When the teachers were asked at one of our meetings, what makes an effective teacher, we all answered the more obvious skills, planning and so on, but the head said we must think about what we do, be aware of the part we play in the school. It's the same for the children. The children do the coffee money, for example, they bring round the birthday cards for people to sign, they organise the games during playtimes. It gives them responsibility. When they operate the switchboard at lunchtime they really operate the switchboard; it's not just pretend with someone standing over them. They play a part in the life of the school, their responsibility is within the school community, it's much more than just responsibility for neat book work.'

Wednesday

Occasionally someone from outside who has promised to take an assembly lets them down. Then Neil Hawkes steps in. You would expect him to be able to draw on many past assemblies and indeed he can. Today he is going to take an Infant assembly with nothing at all prepared, and not only has the promised assembly leader not turned up, so neither has the pianist.

'Oh well,' says Mr Hawkes wryly, 'here goes!', and he sets off to fix up the tape recorder and sit contemplatively in the hall.

It is a smaller group than usual, composed entirely of the youngest children. They come in and sit down as usual without speaking, placing themselves in the more intimate arrangement of a semi-circle. The head congratulates them on coming in quietly and announces that they will sing *Come let us remember the joys of the town* and Louise Conroy volunteers herself for the piano. 'Thank you very much Mrs Conroy!' says Neil Hawkes, visibly relieved. Shirley Ball leads the singing with great gusto and the song has a delightful energy.

Neil Hawkes takes on a Bible story. ('Does anyone know what a Bible is? See if you can find a Bible in your home.') It's the story of Naman. Mr

Hawkes says, 'Naman was a soldier, big and strong, fair, a good man, he co-operated with people.' This month, co-operation is the value word so it has to be brought in to the conversation whenever possible. A small boy is selected from several volunteers to come out and take the part of Naman. The head teacher continues, 'But Naman has a secret illness. It's a skin problem, one we don't get here. It's called lep-ro-sy.'

The disease is explained as one that people were frightened of long ago in Biblical times but that is not a problem any more, and the story moves on. Neil Hawkes asks for a girl to volunteer to play the part of Naman's wife, several very small girls refuse (they're new this term, apparently), then one stands up and comes out to the centre of the hall. However, when he needs another girl for the servant, several eager hands go up. Naman goes to see the prophet Elisha, is told to wash in the river, 'not once but seven times – we don't wash ourselves seven times when we have a bath, do we, but that's what Naman had to do!' Naman is miraculously cured. By this time children represent all the characters mentioned in the tale and are standing in a semi-circular group in the middle of the hall around Mr Hawkes. Naman and his wife hold hands when the cure is made.

Neil Hawkes Then Naman went home and told everyone about it. You must trust and love God, that's what Naman said, and that's what we must do.

There is a prayer of thanks, and a wish that the world would be a happy place, then a birthday announcement – it's Isaac's seventh and he speaks enthusiastically of the prospect of going to McDonald's with his friends. It is all lovely. However, there is one more thing to say. There has been an unusual hiatus in the form of a minor stone-throwing incident, breaking some glass of a house next to the school, and Mr Hawkes has decided after a moment or two's hesitation that he must mention it, although in general the positive medium of the assembly is not used for disciplinary matters. The incident is explained.

Neil Hawkes When stones are thrown they always hurt something. So what would I want you to do with stones?

Boy Not pick them up.

Neil Hawkes Yes. Put your hands up if you understand.

They are ready to conclude. Dolphin music is put on the tape, a little girl starts to cry and climbs on Louise Conroy's lap; explaining that she thought the sounds the dolphins were making meant that they were being hurt.

Mr Hawkes They're not hurt! That's how they talk to each other. They're just talking.

The following term there was a sequel to this assembly at harvest festival, when the elderly neighbours whose glass had suffered were invited back 'to see another side of us'. It was a beautiful occasion. The entire school was packed into the hall, with the visitors seated at the back. A huge table in the corner of the hall was laden with fruit and vegetables and tins of food. Gentle music was played on the piano. The children filed in as usual, but because the whole school came it took ten minutes and a bit of engineering to seat them. Neil Hawkes welcomed the visitors and children's heads began to turn so he said gently, 'Please stay facing the front, it's no fun to be stared at.' The children turned back again and the assembly continued.

Neil Hawkes spoke of his recent visit to Mauritius (speaking for UNICEF about the values programme), the growing of sugar cane and the curved axes used to harvest it before it was boiled and put in bags to send to Sainsbury's.

'It's been a good year, this year,' said Mr Hawkes, 'people are having parties and thanking God for the harvest.' He had met many different people – Chinese, African – working happily together. At a signal, a pupil brought him a prop: a plate with a red apple, a green apple and a knife. The apples were shown to the children, pretty, attractive fruits, good for us, different in appearance on the outside – the children craned to see – but when cut in half, the same inside. 'That's like people,' said Neil Hawkes, 'we're all the same inside, we all have the same sort of feelings – happiness, sadness, excitement perhaps. People all over the world are the same inside.' Time was given to the consideration of food. 'Where does food come from?' Some scattered replies. 'Where does milk come from?' 'The milkman.' Laughter.

'We need to remember that in some countries people, the grown-ups and the children, grow the food, and that some of them have nothing at all to eat when the crops fail. We need especially to remember the Sudan.' Next, while *Ave Maria* was played on the piano, each class sent an emissary with a small basket of fruit. The gifts were received with thanks and added to the store. The Infants sang *See the farmer sow the seed* and the Juniors led the whole school in *Lord of the Harvest*, a hymn-style song lustily sung. 'Let us give thanks now to God, in nature revealed,' said the head teacher, 'and for this fine display. Keep your wonderful patience going while you're going out!' And they did, through a near ten-minute disembarkation from the hall, having sat in a crowded room and concentrated and sung for just over half an hour, the five-year-olds right up to the top Juniors.

The elderly visitors said they found it 'touching' and 'moving'. They said they were amazed at the total concentration, they applauded the explanation of the different people – 'the apple story was very good' – they said they loved living near the school and enjoyed the children's proximity so much that in the school holidays they missed them. But, hadn't there been a bit of a contretemps with some stones last term?

'Oh it was nothing really,' said one of the elders. 'A storm in a teacup. We've all got grandchildren, we understand these things can happen. The mistake was in laying a gravel path in the first place; children are bound to pick up bits of it. Boys will, anyhow.' The others agreed that the incident had been well handled and that the harm done had been little and understandable. You could almost have thought the stones had been put down to test the children, and that it wasn't quite a fair test.

Assembly planning

And now back to the Infants assembly at which the incident was first introduced. Neil Hawkes concluded it and left the hall. In his own room he said, 'Was that all right? A wing and a prayer, I had nothing ready you know, not a thing.' Of course, the remark was disingenuous. He has been planning and holding assemblies for years and years, and has an encyclopaedia of material in his head. Moreover, record sheets of the Acts of Worship have to be kept, and he has them all filed along with the source material in his office. The record sheet for 2 June looks like this, all in different-coloured pens:

Theme: Blindness

Month's value: Trust

Learning intention: To develop empathy for people with the condition of blindness.

Worship outline: We may be able to see and yet have inner blindness.

(c.f. my assemblies 5.6.95 and 3.6.96)

Next there is a chart, a complicated web of ideas, leading out on lines from the central cloud entitled blindness. The strands of thought run:

- picture three dogs –

- recognise blind people – physical condition – mental e.g. 'oh, you must be blind', i.e. not understanding –

- what is it? – experience – feely bag Key Stage 1 – sit in silence – eyes closed –

- are we all blind? new ideas –

- overcoming blindness – Louis Braille –

Then Trust comes into the chart.

- Who do we trust? Why? What is Trust? – and leads directly to:

- Jesus helps us to see how we should behave in life, two golden rules, love God and love your neighbour as yourself.

Further notes accompany the web and develop some of the ideas, for example:

- we still have our inner eye – imagination, to visualise with. c.f. person born blind.

- the ability to use imagination, a great gift – e.g. keep a happy/peaceful picture in your imagination when life gets difficult. Use waterfall experience, p.167 *Values and Visions* to create a moment of peace, to feel calm, to use the inner eye of the imagination to see what is important.

On the back of the record sheet is the Waterfall visualization:

With each breath let your body become more and more relaxed. With each out breath, breathe out any worry … with each in breath feel yourself breathing in quietness and calm.

Now imagine a beautiful waterfall of light entering the top of your head … feel the waterfall of light gently flowing through your head … down your neck … into your chest and shoulders. The waterfall of light is warm and full of gentle energy … feel it move down your shoulders … into your arms … your hands and out through your fingers. More light falls as a waterfall down your back … into your tummy … your legs … down to your feet and out through your toes … washing away with it any stress or worry.

Now you are completely bathed in a continuous waterfall of light … enjoy its freshness and the gentle calm it brings … in a moment you are going to leave the waterfall of light and you will find yourself back in the hall, feeling relaxed, calm and refreshed … when you are ready, open your eyes.

The last element in the assembly plan is a reflection.

Dear God, help us to understand the difficulties that people have who have no sight. May we never take our sight for granted. Also, help us to develop our inner sight of imagination and understanding so that we may never be blind to the needs of others or ourselves. Amen.

A further assembly plan

An important assembly for seven- to nine-year-olds on the subject of family was given a few years ago and has been adapted for use a few times since. The thought strands leading out from the central idea are these:

- parents – children – differences – all families are different

- wider meaning – family: school – community, country, world!

- Neil photos – family

- children – Stephen – Gary – show pictures – talk

- feelings – learning – life – importance – love? – upset

- behaviour – respect – tolerance

- us – God – family – works through us – Noah – change world better

- Peace game – better world chart

- responses – family – behaviour

And the reflection:

Let us keep very still and think about the people who make up our family. Let us remember that life in our family should be loving, caring and respectful. Our relationships within our family act as the foundations for the relationships we have with all the others who make up our world family. So with God's help and our own determination, each one of us can make a better world.

Thursday

The school assembly has to fulfil a multitude of functions. On Thursdays there is the birthday assembly, when everyone in Infants whose birthday falls during that week is given a birthday card by the head teacher. They step out and receive their cards, and birthday stickers, and at the end of the summer term great patience was demanded of the assembled children because Sean, Rebecca, Lauren, Gemma, Chloe, Elise, Emma, Daniel, Jordan, Natasha, Matthew, Lindsay, Lewis, Charlotte, Kirsty, Kayley, Hayley, Ben, Lewis, Laurence, Tom, Philippa, Lee and Aran, all had birthdays either at the end of term or in prospect in the holidays. All were greeted and congratulated, and stood up and came out to receive a card and a sticker, and the lines had to be rearranged a couple of times to fit them all in.

'Well done for the patient way we're doing this,' said the head. He congratulated the waiting children on their patience rather than exhorting them to keep silent for a few more minutes. He did this in just the same way that he would congratulate the whole school on the cleanliness of the toilets if he wanted to ensure that any errant children stopped messing them up. The emphasis used in the toilets question is the same as the emphasis for assembly behaviour and all other disciplinary matters: positive, since the preferred method is always to praise excellence rather than chastise error. The autistic boy whispered a bit and was quietened, and at last they all sang their birthday song which is not *Happy Birthday to You,* but one with the chorus:

> Strong to do right,
> Slow to do wrong,
> And thoughtful for others,
> All the day long.

The Thursday before that one there had only been about three birthdays, which left time for quite a long conversation about pets, which even featured a large, live star: Charlie the dog, making a personal appearance in the school hall having been brought in from the head teacher's home. 'What do pets give to us? What do we notice about them?' A different situation also needed attention, that of the preliminary visit of next term's new pupils, most of whom were sitting in the assembly with their parents, looking tentative. They were gently welcomed and at the end of the meeting the children went to spend half an hour in their next year's classrooms while their parents were briefed by the head in the staff room. 'Bring your hankies on the first day,' he told the parents, 'but don't worry about the children. They'll be much less tearful than you are!'

He remarks privately that visitors tend to think the assembly is easy and relaxed. 'Actually,' he says, 'it looks easy and relaxed but for it to be like that requires a lot of hard work. They see the children filing in quietly, they don't know that it's not from being shouted at but because they've been shown how to do it and because of the expectation that they will be like that. There's a lot in the expectation.'

Friday

There is also the children's own assembly, which one or other class does on Fridays. It is very popular with the children during their time at the school and is remembered with pleasure by the ones who have left. It follows the pattern of song and play and poems, omitting only the reflection. The critical difference is that the children run it themselves with no help from their class teacher – with whom, however, they will have discussed it. It is said not to take up much rehearsal time since the material the children use is more or less what they are working on anyway.

Year Threes, for example, gave an assembly on the theme of co-operation and have brought a playlet of a three-legged race which went very badly until a child came on and urged the participants to co-operate, whereupon they set off running together properly instead of pulling against each another. First the whole assembly sang *I can see clearly now the rain has gone*, with the tape recorder, then the word co-operation was spelled out in the American manner. 'Gimme a C', cried the first child in the line. The assembled children shouted 'C!' and the child held up a large paper C. 'Gimme an O!', cried the next. 'O' they cried – and so on.

At the beginning of the autumn term, a class assembly given to the whole school on unity echoed the one on co-operation. It began after a delay of about five minutes caused by one of the teachers who was trying to video it and had a camera problem. The children sat silently and patiently throughout this hiccup. One of the teachers remarked later that she only realised how marvellous this had been a week later when she recalled her other schools, 'We'd have been hauling them out to the front, shouting at them, there'd have been talking and laughing. You don't realise how different it is here, it's another world. I can't even remember what it's like to teach in any other school.'

At last the camera was fixed and the signal given for the children to start the assembly. Two of them stood at the front of the hall.

Child 1 Good morning! Have you ever been lonely?

Child 2 Sometimes it might be your own fault!

Child 1 Here are two stories.

Child 2 The first one is 'The bee who wanted to be different.'

There followed two playlets. In the first, a group of children dressed as bees applied themselves to the job of making a honeycomb with hexagonal pieces of paper representing the cells. However, one bee wanted to cut her paper in a different shape.

Bee 1 (wilfully) I don't want to make six-sided cells!

Bee 2 (co-operating) You can't do it like that!

Teacher Bee You'll have to take that cell out and make it the other way.

Bee 1 No!

The irregular cell could not be fitted into the honeycomb and the wilful bee had to leave the hive, to her immense surprise and sorrow.

Child 1 When people or creatures want to live together, they must fit in.

In story two, the population of a village attended four different churches, and the members of the separate congregations didn't speak to each other. A new family came to the village, whose members divided themselves between the denominations. This caused problems for the villagers, who found it impossible to decide which members of the family to talk to. Worse was to come. A storm (beautifully conveyed with sound effects made entirely by the seated children) damaged the roof of the chapel. There was nothing for it but for all the villagers to help mend the roof, which they did, and departed shaking hands.

Mr Hawkes came to the front, congratulated the children and spoke up for the oddball bee. 'I think they probably let her back in,' he said. There were some useful remarks on the subject of doing things as a joint effort and doing them individually, with a recommendation for understanding. Unity had been cleverly shown simultaneously to mean fitting the pattern and accepting differences for the sake of happy co-existence, a sophisticated near-paradox. Next the children who form the School Council gave certificates to various children to reward positive characteristics: a caring attitude, helpfulness, always having a smile on her face. Each certificate-holder was congratulated by Neil Hawkes, who endorsed all the qualities.

At the end of assemblies the children are invited to give notices or announcements and usually several of them in turn give information about the life of the school. They may announce a local or school event, or a fund-raising activity. They simply get up from their row, walk to the front of the hall, make their announcement clearly, go back to their place and sit down again, without fuss or organisation from adults.

Neil Hawkes believes this practice is on the increase. 'Nowadays, more children are giving notices at the end of assembly than adults. I think it's fantastic, it makes a very positive feeling about us, about the community. There's a powerful message in allowing children to do that. And it isn't just the extroverts doing it, some of the shyest children do it too. The way they feel confident enough to get up and talk somehow says something about the school. It has to do with the way they see this as a school for all of us. They also know if they say something it has to be something of quality, they don't just get up for the sake of talking. The intensity with which the children listen to other children is extraordinary and very pleasing and I'm sure it's partly because the adults also are exemplifying great joy – and really listening to the children. The children sense it and it gives them courage.'

It happened that an observer from abroad was at this children's assembly. 'What's wonderful about this,' he said, 'is the way the theme ties into the whole ethos. It means the children are running their own, whole-school ethos, they're taking responsibility for it themselves. They're actually put in charge of maintaining their own ethos. Also the way the School Council runs the community means they take responsibility for the community.'

He is not the first to remark on these two important factors: the consistency of outlook and the level of responsibility taken by the children. After all, in how many schools do children conduct their own assemblies? (And conduct them, it has to be said, without self-consciousness or shyness?) This accords with the way the children run the office at lunchtime. They are shown what to do and how to do it and then entrusted with doing it properly. The response in both cases is a very professional job. The children's assemblies are held by the children. The teachers bring their classes to the assembly hall in silence according to custom, but no one starts off the proceedings except the children, no one operates an overhead projector or a tape recorder except the children: the event is their own. The confidence this gives them in their own presentation skills is yet another plus.

Class assemblies

At the end of the summer term Louise Conroy held several of her class assemblies on the subject of journeys, with particular reference to the following school year. Here the class assembly was being used, as it quite often is, to help towards an understanding of the life changes affecting the children. Her class was going up and they were writing and talking about it and recalling their year in her class, thus journeys began in the class assembly and continued into the class work. The children had brought pictures of themselves as babies and stuck them on the board at the front of the room, and they were trying to guess which of the babies had become whom in the class. Some of them read their essays about being in the next year group. 'I will be happy to be in Miss Pack's class and I will be sad to leave Louise Conroy's class,' wrote one of the girls.

They had written about the journey from being seven to eight years old. 'When I was in Year Two I could not do tens and units. My handwriting was appalling, now it's good,' said one child. 'I couldn't do my tables, didn't join up my letters,' said another. Seven-year-old April had written a letter to Mrs Conroy from the preceding class, it had a border decorated with pictures of herself and the legend: 'I'm excited'. She gave herself a glowing reference. 'In my report it said a lot of nice things like April is a delightful member of the class so I hope I am a delightful member of the class for you.' However, there was a caveat. 'But can I ask you a question? Do you give the children hard work? But when you try to answer that question I would like you to be OHNEST (sic).' It would appear that one at least of the value words had been well understood. At the end of her letter, April offered more information. 'PS my sir name is Wyatt. And when I'm older I'd like to be a hairdresser.'

Louise Conroy spoke of her own life journey, which had reached a crossroads the preceding Easter when she got married. The transitions in her own life were related to the way in which the children were moving up the school.

What some of the staff think

'You find that you open up about yourself here, much more than usual,' says Louise Conroy. She believes that more is required of the teachers but the experience is entirely enriching. As an illustration she offers, 'My whole class and most of the school choir came to my wedding, and all their parents did too! It's very giving – and you have to give a lot in return. It's very equal, the expectations are very equal. Because I give a lot, they give a lot.' Furthermore, it's a big family, this school. My class, we see ourselves as a family within the community. It brings responsibilities.'

John Heppenstall has taught at the school for some 20 years and remembers previous styles. He believes the current policy on assemblies is energising. 'The influence of the assembly is very important,' he says. 'We used to have fewer, and they weren't used to promote the ethos. There's a great knock-on effect in the way we do them now. The playground behaviour is better, there's more co-operation, less bad language. School assembly is to do with leadership, and one of the effects of various people taking assemblies is that the leadership is spread.'

For his part, Neil Hawkes says the phenomenon of teachers taking assemblies shows the success of informality within the structure. 'Because we have a similar philosophy we pick up intuitively what each other is doing – and also we can fill gaps swiftly if they appear.' He does not underestimate his own part in the transformation of the school assembly into a kind of meeting that performs many functions and welds the whole together. 'Assemblies are the main vehicle for me to have a major influence on the school,' he says, 'I can influence them, staff as well as children, through the assembly. The big role of the head teacher is to be a leader, not only in school but also in the community. And the big quality is to be definite. There should be no ambiguity.

'Our assemblies create the climate for everyone to reach their inner space. The point is in not constraining. The traditional school assembly actively stops children from getting to that point within themselves.'

The tone of the school is set in assembly, and permeates the curriculum and all the activities inside and outside it. Far from thinking of abandoning the school assembly, West Kidlington School knows it to be the cornerstone.

THE KIDLINGTON BLUEPRINT

Many parents talk through aspects of their children's day – and their own. Mrs Gardner says in Chapter Seven that she asks her children at tea time about events at school or play group, first in general and then in particular. What were the bad things and what were the good things? What did they most enjoy? How will they make tomorrow better? What are they looking forward to? Together they look at how things went at school and at work, and how things might be improved. They always emphasise and celebrate the good things.

Contributing thoughts on the events of a day brings families together. Contributing thoughts in the light of a value word brings another dimension. How did our trip to the zoo bring in the idea of friendship – responsibility – trust – or whatever is your current family word? How did our trip to the cinema affect our thoughts? How did the value concept come into a television programme we watched together, or perhaps, which of the characters best embodied it?

The school assembly is an extremely enjoyable tool in the positive effort. You can copy a powerful part of it at home. At least once or twice a week, ideally on the same day/s and at the same time, sit quietly together. Lead up to a minute or two of silent contemplation of your value word. It will help everyone to feel and be more centred, more in touch with their positive, essential, inner self. It will bring calm, self-esteem and self-knowledge. It will strengthen each member of the family and the family community.

The practice of stopping all activity and giving time to be still in the midst of activity for two or three minutes several times a day is also invaluable. Consider how you are feeling and whether you want to feel different. It may come as a surprise to know that you have a choice. Once you have learned the technique of slowing down and observing your situation you will gain command of it – and of yourself.

CHAPTER 6

Children Talking

THE CHILDREN OF WEST KIDLINGTON SCHOOL SPEAK AS EASILY TO ADULTS as they do to each other, and as easily to children of different ages as to those of their own age. They are confident but never cheeky; they have proper respect but are never cowed (although there is sometimes shyness). They take part in most of their conversations in a considered way, without getting overheated or trying to take over. It has been noted elsewhere that they hold doors open for people as a matter of course, and say please and thank you and behave considerately.

The children's good manners come from a genuine understanding of how to create harmony, and the practice of them gives the children great freedom. This quality is useful in conversation and communication too. They can ask for information or request what they need from adults; they can say what they want and how they feel in ways that find constructive response. Adults comment on how delightful they are to deal with and what a pleasure it is to do things for them. People attending assertiveness training courses may wish they had the skills of West Kidlington pupils! It follows that the children make friends easily. They settle disputes between themselves, they know how to negotiate terms and how to apologise if necessary. They have also been taught to play with any children who have been left out, and they do it for the most part very willingly. They are unusually sensitive to one another's moods and needs.

The work on developing confidence and articulacy starts at the beginning of their school lives. The ethos of the school and the way the children are treated in class, the way they participate in assemblies, in particular their own assemblies, which they hugely enjoy, all contribute to personal strength and to a fluent and balanced mode of expression. This is enjoyable for other people and invaluable to the children, many of whom appreciate what their early schooling has done for them. This essay was written by eleven-year-old Katherine Thackray as she was leaving the school.

'At West Kidlington School we have a values policy. It consists of a different value each month which we concentrate on and learn about to help us with our futures. I believe it has taught us to be well-behaved, good mannered, anti-racist and to have a good attitude. Some of the most recent values have been care, kindness, happiness, and humility, which is our current one. It teaches us to be humble and to be a good loser. Another of our values was quality, and Mr Hawkes, our head teacher, insists that our work is of high quality and we think and act with thought. So far this is happening, or so say all the visitors we get, which I agree with. From my point of view the change in our school has been phenomenal. We have had no serious behaviour problems, actually there have been no problems at all. Also there has been no vandalism, racism or any other problems. So the values work we have been doing at our school has helped us a great deal, so we should turn out to be good, law-abiding adults.'

And it is a safe bet that they will be good, law-abiding adults who nevertheless are full of life, imagination and enterprise.

Two years into her secondary schooling Katherine remembers her primary schooldays happily and says they still affect her outlook a great deal. She recalls the beginnings of the daily practice of reflection during assembly.

'I remember the reflection being very settling and relaxing. We did deep breathing and imagined things like walking across a meadow barefoot, and every time you breathed out, you imagined breathing out your problems. I started the day at peace, I felt very calm and I think it's quite useful. I think it's good to do it for a short time, you can't do it for too long, the Infants especially wouldn't be able to stay still. It's nice doing it in the morning, I think it made people more mature, more level-headed.

'I was about nine when we first started doing it and at the time I thought it was a bit strange. Everyone else thought so too but we all joined in. Actually everyone quite enjoyed it but we didn't want to say so, some of us made a front [pretended] but really we liked it. If you had problems it made them seem better and you could see different ways of working them out. We always had slow, easy music. One I particularly liked was the dolphin sounds one. I bought the CD, it helps you go to sleep.

'I remember telling my friends about it. They're twins, they're at a different school and they thought we were weird! They said, "you'll be hugging trees next!" – but really it's very useful. We used to do a similar thing at the end of PE lessons in the hall. You've been really buzzing, running around, then it calms you down so you can go into your next lesson. Actually I miss it now.

'People from West Kidlington who are now at my secondary school are well-behaved, but some of the others can be disruptive. They're expecting not to enjoy themselves, I think that's why, they're expecting they'll get shouted at. I expect to learn something – I start by thinking, what will be fun in lessons, what will I find interesting? We come in ready to enjoy the lessons. I don't think any lessons are boring, it's just what you make of them.

'I think some of the teachers at my new school have been hardened by the disruptive ones [pupils]. Teachers might think when they meet you, "Will she be mouthy?" but if you talk to them nicely they talk to you nicely back. But it's very different at secondary school. I thought some of the other pupils were quite wild, I was shocked by their behaviour and attitude. But then, no secondary school could be the same as what I had at primary school.

'Sometimes I thought the values lessons at West Kidlington were a bit silly, but they were useful when you were given a situation and asked what should this person have done. It makes you think about different situations and how to handle them, and you see that there's always more than one way of doing it. Now I often find I go back in my mind to West Kidlington and work things out like we did then. It's a bit like an Encarta program – you feed in the problem and you get some solutions out. You try one and if that doesn't work you try another. It works if you're calm. When we reflected I used to think about the problems of the day before and wonder if I could have done something better.

'At my new school if I have fall-outs with my friends I might want to run off and say, "*all right, be like that!*" – but I know I must talk about it and compromise. Honesty's better. One of the good things at West Kidlington is they'd always involve the older ones in the playground to talk things out and it made it easier because you were talking to someone nearer your own age. I'm sure the Infants would find it easier to talk to a pupil.

'When I did the playground monitoring I liked having the responsibility, to tell you the truth I was quite proud of myself. I thought, "I'm very grown up, they'll come and ask me things now!" It was satisfying sorting out problems and – you might think is funny – I used to act as if I was an adult. When I did the office duty I really liked answering the phone, I sounded really grown up. People used to say, "the children are very sensible," and it made you more mature and grown-up. You had to think about what you were going to do.

'Teaching all these values meant a lot of things. One thing was, the brighter people [pupils] used to support people who didn't understand things in class. That's nice, I think now I'm at another school some people probably don't help other people as much as they could. At West Kidlington the atmosphere made you concentrate on the work more. We were bright, I think because everyone's happy and calm they're learning more. It's a shame I couldn't have been there longer.

'I think the children at my old school have been taught to be more mature and I think that helps – otherwise little children are too shy to ask questions. At my new school I say if I don't understand. I'm at ease with the teachers, really you can almost speak to them like friends. There's less, "Yes, sir!"– you can drop the formality. I think we find some things easier because of our primary school. Me and another girl from my year were asked to show some visitors round my new school. I didn't mind, I made an effort to make them feel welcome. I actually found it easy but I noticed she only answered the questions they asked, she seemed quite shy.

'All those things, everything we did really, made people use their values. What did I like best about my primary school? I liked the whole lot!'

Year Six on the values programme

Here are four school leavers. They are ten or eleven years old and have spent nearly six years at primary school; they are the seniors who are about to become the youngest juniors at their new schools. It happens that these six years have been the years of the introduction of the values programme, so they were there from its inception. They are bright, articulate and optimistic, but naturally the prospect of the leap into a new school is daunting. Some of them (and many of their parents) say they wish West Kidlington would let them stay until they are eighteen! They were asked what they liked best about it.

Clare Playtimes! I like talking to my friends, with no one asking for answers to things like they do in lessons.

Lizzie I like assemblies. Mr Hawkes talks about values. He has a way of explaining it that makes you understand.

Clare Doesn't bore you.

Mark He puts everything into stories. He tells his own experiences but you can put your hand up if you have something to say. When we were doing courage I owned up to things I've done and it didn't matter, nobody minded. I owned up to lots of things.

Clare Mr Hawkes makes it [religious stories] interesting, he reads it properly, he puts in a lot of enthusiasm and he sometimes changes it round. Sometimes we have to find out where things have come from or who said them. He says we're Bible detectives. It makes it sound fun, makes me want to go and find out.

Lizzie He seems interested in us. I mean interested in all of us. We're doing simplicity now and he makes it so interesting I feel as if it's just me in the room.

Clare I missed simplicity and I don't really understand it and I really mind! I might never understand it.

On the morning of the assembly explaining the concept of simplicity Clare had travelled the 55 miles to Birmingham to be interviewed by Central Television about the forthcoming local elections. She would have much preferred to go to school assembly. The children find the value words engrossing and often say so and it is perhaps a measure of how interesting they find them that Clare would rather have gone to school assembly than appear on television. The conversation moved to how the words affect their behaviour.

Mark We play hockey in a group from school and we always stop the game if anyone's hurt. If anybody falls over or hurts themselves we look after them. We try not to get in people's way and we don't kick anybody or anything like that. We show more values than boys from other schools. Some of us were playing last week, all of them [were] from here except one boy from another school we play with sometimes. At first he was pushing and kicking and playing rough but then he saw that's not how we play and he stopped it. We said, 'we don't play like that.' (Something in this incident reminded Mark of his friend Sam.) Sam was a terror before values education! He used to lead a gang.

Lizzie You were a demon child! There's a demon child in a story we've been doing and he's just like Sam used to be.

Mark He's changed a lot.

Sam We still have rows.

Mark Yeah, but not *real* rows. We don't get angry. If we have a row we just don't talk for a day. Then we forget not to talk, like at going home time we're friends again because we've forgotten we're not meant to be talking. We don't keep it up.

The four children agreed that disputes should be settled quickly.

Clare We're telepathic, we know when people are upset! I always know when my friend's upset before she says anything.

Mark You shouldn't have an argument, you should just walk away.

Just walking away is a West Kidlington mainstay in situations when something dodgy might be about to start, and when they go on to secondary schools that is what the West Kidlington children do when necessary. The talk moved to the prospect of secondary school. Sam had seen teenagers misbehaving. His concerns were listed in ascending order of dreadfulness.

Sam Some boys were smoking behind the pub, I saw them. They were smoking and I saw them throwing things. [Hushed tones] *And they were rude to their teachers!*

Mark Wasting!

Sam They need someone to talk to. Someone should find out why they're doing it. There must be something wrong.

107

Assumptions: first, that problems can be resolved by discussion; second, that the misbehaving teenagers need help. Then values in general became the topic.

Mark Sometimes I just think about values.

Sam You can't just *think* about values, it's got to be something you're concerned about. It's different every time something different happens, you have to make it mean something according to what's happening. You have to see if values can help you work it out.

Lizzie I pray a lot.

Clare Values come into your life.

Lizzie I've got the whole room full of cuddly toys. I've got about 40. I have a favourite one for a week at a time so they all get a turn. Sometimes at night when I'm in bed I snuggle down with my cuddly toy and think about the day, remember it, and think about the value.

The practice last thing at night of recalling the positive elements of the day, and concluding with the positive value of the moment, has been taught in assembly.

Mark Sometimes I use [value] words in arguments. I say to Johnny [his twin], don't have a go! He tries to wind me up and I say: be *calm!* ....Well, it *sometimes* works.

Lizzie I talk to my mum a lot, she's my best friend. She still tells me a bedtime story, she's reading me the *Diary of Anne Frank* at the moment. We tell each other everything. Since values education I get on with her better. I've learnt values and I'm more tolerant now.

The use of value words such as tolerant is frequent and unconscious, demonstrating the accuracy of the suggestion that they are the reference points that form the children's behavioural framework. Between the children, concern about secondary school resurfaces.

Clare [to Lizzie] You'll be all right, your personality is nice and people will like you.

Lizzie It helps me to solve problems if I can think how people would feel if I did the same to them. That's what I'll do, I'll think about it from the other side.

Sam Values makes you more independent. You've got courage and hope inside yourself and you don't need people. You can be friends with people and you like them but you don't need them.

Mark I think values affects friendships. You can be friends with more people. You're more confident, you're more kind and helpful and people like it. People like you better because you're nicer.

Lizzie Values makes you more organised.

By 'more organised', perhaps Lizzie meant that the positive values work brings clarity of thought and expression. These children have great capacity for introspection and empathy. They have an objective viewpoint and orderly minds. They also have the means of working things out for themselves or, if they cannot, of finding someone to help them.

Neil Hawkes says the values work raises consciousness. 'They don't think in a situation, "here I must use the value of honesty" – it just comes naturally,' he says. However Sam, Clare, Lizzie and Mark can also refer consciously to their positive values. In social situations such as the football game or a potential dispute with a friend they can see how what they do is affected by the principles they have learnt.

Neil Hawkes talking to Year Six children

Neil Hawkes What would you tell a visitor to the school about why values are taught?

Debbie We do values so we aren't horrible to others, and don't feel bad about ourselves. It means you have more friends. I spoke to the Swedish people [visitors] at the pond area and they asked how it was for us when we were working together. I said I found it was easier because we had the value of co-operation. And also, if you do something wrong, you'll know how to correct it.

Mara We learn about values so we can become better people – otherwise the world won't be a very good place. In the past people have not really thought about anything like this and, they sort of, don't care about anything. I'd say to a visitor that we have got to behave because of our values.

Nial Values improve our life. You become a kinder pupil, we listen and we can concentrate. We can really think about what we do in different circumstances. It also helps because the whole school can be united. I told a visitor about our assemblies and how we understand the value words.

Tom We learn values because it gives a chance to get more out of life, be more loving to our friends and our families, and then we'll pass it on to the next generation. I told visitors we like values and it helps us to have a nice feeling.

Neil Hawkes Do you enjoy learning about values?

Debbie I enjoy it because it's fun. At first I didn't understand it but now each time we have a new experience I learn something new. It is like opening up a new way of life.

Mara I like it because I find it interesting and I want to be a better person when I go to my secondary school. I don't like horrible people.

Nial I quite like the stories and then we have to write them out. It gives us something to think about and something to share with the others in your class.

Tom It gives you something, like at playtime we all play well together and think about what we have learnt. I went out when we had been taught about patience and we were having a little talk about what we should try and we found that everyone was finding out what others wanted to do and taking it in turns. It was very successful.

Neil Hawkes Has learning about values helped you?

Debbie I've learned that if you do your best, it's OK. You can't be right all the time but it doesn't matter as long as you're trying hard. If you are doing your best that's good enough for anybody, it's as much as you can do.

Mara It's given me a better attitude. For example, I'm learning the violin and sometimes when I can't get it right I might have thought of giving up, but now because of values I think I've got to be positive and try and crack it. I could have stopped but I wanted to carry on because although it was hard I wanted to do it.

Nial I try to be a kinder person. I used to argue or have a go at people and I don't do that any more. I don't argue any more because I do not like arguing.

Tom If I didn't know about values I would not be such a nice person to know. I think that children put a lot of effort into learning about values and being nice. I am not saying that other people cannot be nice, because they can, but it makes life easier if you know about values and it really comes more naturally to be nice.

Neil Hawkes Do you think you have been helped to think differently because of learning about values?

Debbie If someone says something horrible I might have retaliated but now I think they might have a reason. At Atlantic College [school outdoor holiday week] we had a misunderstanding and we learned that you understand what other people are thinking before you react.

Mara I think about people's feelings and how they would think if I said something horrible.

Tom Learning values helps me to concentrate and look at deep meanings in things.

Neil Hawkes Have your parents or other people noticed any differences because of the values programme?

Debbie My mum notices because I'm more helpful! Now if there's something that needs doing at home, like washing the dishes, I'll say, Oh, OK, I'll do that.

Mara My parents think I'm better at keeping my temper.

Tom My grandparents always know which word we're doing. They always say you've been learning about – this word – recently, haven't you? So I must be doing things they notice.

Year Five on the values programme

Here are Lindsay, Joseph, Peter, Annie and Lucy considering similar questions: their favourite school activities, how they learned the value words, when they refer to them and what effects they can see. Like Sam, Lizzie, Clare and Mark, they find the values work interesting. There is great security in the shared effort.

Lindsay My favourite thing at school? I quite like learning things. Most things. Art's best.

Peter I like maths. My grandad's a mathematician and my mum's good at maths and she taught me before I came to school. She still helps me.

Joseph I like English and I like painting pictures.

Lucy My best lesson is science. I like experiments. I like learning how things are made up, like a dandelion or parts of flowers. I like seeing how it works.

Annie My favourite lesson is sewing; I drew a parrot [on to tapestry canvas] and now I'm sewing it.

The children's own forthcoming assembly was occupying their minds.

Lindsay Every Friday a class has an assembly of its own. Plays and things. It's us next week, I'm nervous!

Lucy The five-year-olds don't do so much so they don't get so nervous. They just say some of the things and their teacher does their readings for them. When you're young you don't realise what you're doing, anyway, so you don't know to get nerves. When you get nerves it's only when you're older because you think you might forget what you've got to say or people will be looking at you.

Annie I've got to play a piece of music. It's a Grade 2 piece, it's meant to be relaxing. Well, it is relaxing. It's for simplicity. We all do different sections of the assembly.

Joseph I'm narrating. I've learned everything I've got to say by heart. Our assembly is about simplicity, it's about looking at life in a different way.

The children were asked what simplicity meant.

Joseph Oh, that's difficult ... It's beautiful ... Simplicity is beautiful. it means staying in the present, economy, using resources wisely, not wasting things, not being careless, giving time to your friends. I've missed some out but that's what I think it means.

Lucy We've been shown how simplicity is, how we can live better lives. Small things can make a difference. Like, if you did something for a person, even if it was somebody you didn't know, it changes things.

Joseph In Year Three when I was being bullied I went to Mr Hawkes and he told me to stay calm and focused and try and ignore it. I had to use values in a way, but really that was even before the values started.

The whole values programme had only been in place for a couple of years at the time of this conversation and these children had therefore passed their earliest schooldays without its full vigour. Staying calm and focused was one of the early exercises.

Lucy You do the basic ones in Infants.

Annie Like honesty.

Lucy We had the words on a piece of paper [display card], then we had a story with the words in.

Annie Love was first.

Joseph It was kindness, wasn't it?

Lucy If there's something going on, they [the value words] help us. The teachers tell us how to use them. When we were doing humility everyone was all quiet and no one got into rows. Even when we went home, when Mum and Dad spoke to us they spoke quietly. For a whole month it was really quiet at home!

Peter How values affect our lives? You learn to respect other people, you don't keep getting into trouble. When I'm out in Oxford I hold doors open for people. They like it, they always say thank you.

Oxford is seven miles from Kidlington and the children were asked what they liked to do when they went there.

Peter Curioxity! [the hands-on children's science museum] I like design technology, I like how things work. I like the crane thing! You can make it lift things and put them down somewhere else.

Can values even come into leisure activities?

Annie If we're somewhere like Laserquest [the sci-fi game environment], if you're on a team you try to help each other. You don't push past people. In Laserquest it's a sort of maze and you all wear suits with flashing lights, you have to shoot other people's lights and there's numbers on them and when all their lights are out, they're out ... But you have to be careful you don't push people.

The children found nothing contradictory in the idea of shooting people politely and said it was just a game. The principle of consideration co-exists with cyberconquest.

Joseph You've got to be sensible in games. In Laserquest you're in a mini-city and there's stairs and you're running up and down all the time, past people. Last time someone on the other team nudged me. Well, you mustn't get mad.

Annie You have to be careful of other people.

Lucy That's right, you have to not push people, and not hurt them. Sometimes when we play games like rounders, everyone wants to bowl. Then you have to control your anger.

The children considered how to choose a bowler by various means, including what seemed to be the fairest, a counting rhyme involving feet which goes: Ibbl Obbl Black Bobble Ibble Obbl OUT! – but which they felt takes too long. Next Annie pursued the topic of fairness in the context of a troubled classmate.

Annie I walk to school with Susan on Tuesdays and Thursdays when I've got my cello. But I want to walk with my other friends on the other days but she still wants to come. She hasn't really got anybody else to walk with, you see, but I don't want to walk to school with her every single day. I've got other friends. But it's difficult because on the other days she still walks behind me so I have to talk to her.

Lindsay Susan gets teased.

Annie They don't like her glasses, they don't like her hair.

Peter Yes, but she goes along with it.

Lucy She feels upset when there's names, when they call her goggle eyes.

Annie People think she's weird, that's because they don't know her.

Lucy Yes, but she'll still talk to people in the playground.

Lindsay And some people play with her.

Linda Heppenstall, the children's class teacher, explained that Susan is indeed somewhat eccentric but that this group of children have appointed themselves her unofficial guardians and largely protect her from the teasing. Though this still seems uncomfortable there is no real bullying at the school and children who attract unwelcome attention appear to find their own means of protection.

Year Two on the values programme

Here Freddie, Joe, Robin, Vava, Jenny and Nicola.

Vava Our school is very nice because there's a pond and a secret garden.

Joe The swimming pool is shut down.

Jenny It's because somebody dropped something heavy in it and it's not safe.

Robin We could have a car boot sale every week!

Joe We could sell the teachers, we'd get £600!

Robin We'd get £100 each!

Though they were animated by the idea of enterprise they were asked for the current value word.

Jenny Trust, I think it's trust. I know what trust means, it's if you trust somebody and they come round to your house and you want a drink or something and you leave them in your bedroom while you go downstairs and you say don't play with my things and you trust them not to play with your toys.

Nicola When Miss goes to the photocopier she has to trust us to be quiet.

Vava Mrs Ball trusts us to carry on with our work without making a fuss.

Robin I don't trust my sister, I told her not to lose my skipping rope and she did and then I lent it her again and she lost it again, three times.

What is your favourite value word?

Joe Simplicity. I like simplicity. It's very calm. Motionless. Something I can do that's simple is ride my bike. I went to Robin's house and tried first, then I thought, there's a bike in the shed! My dad got it out for me and mended it. Now I can do wheelies! To do wheelies is simple.

Another word?

Vava Care. You have to care about yourself not to fall out of a tree. You have to take care. And I care about my friends, if they fall over I get somebody.

Robin I care for my brother, because when I give him bike lessons he falls off and I care, I get mummy.

Those are good answers about how you care for other people, who cares for you?

Nicola My Mummy.

Jenny All my family, some of my friends and all my pets.

Vava Sometimes my pets get my socks. They eat them.

What about another of the special words?

Freddie Trust. I can trust my brother to look after my things, like my Power Ranger. I can trust my Dad to get my bike out without breaking it. I can trust my Mum because she puts my clothes out all the time, every day.

And another?

Vava Respect. It's the same as care, really. It's when people do nice things to you and you do nice things back. You could share your sweets, or not break things. Or you could take care of our world and not throw litter.

Joe Throwing a can out of a car window shows no respect. That means you haven't got any respect. Somebody did that yesterday when I was going home and I told my Mum.

How do you find out what the words mean?

Nicola They tell stories. I like the way they explain it, the stories really explain. We've had two trust stories with Miss Hawkes. [The head teacher's daughter, a trainee teacher.] One was called *First Snow* and the other was called *Helpers*. In *Helpers*, the mum trusted George who was a teenager to look after three children and he trusted one girl to do the washing-up.

Who can you trust? The five children answered almost as one.

Children I can trust my whole family!

These six-year-olds are at the beginning of their positive values under-standing and already they have clear ideas about what the words mean and how they might affect behaviour. They can see that what they do has an effect in the larger world, and they are ready to observe actions such as throwing a can out of a car window with a disapproving eye. They are already taking in the concept of cause and effect and of behaving positively not only for the sake of other people but as a means of getting a positive response for themselves. The use of story and conversation as mechanisms for considering ethical questions is well established.

A pupil audit

The many observers of human development who have said in one way or another, give me a child until he be seven and I will give you the man, are united on this point: early lessons are crucial. The lessons on which these youngest learners are making such a sturdy beginning, of trust, respect, caring, simplicity, and all the rest, are shown to be a strong and truthful focus with which to perceive the world and a sound framework for oper-ating within it.

Year Six questionnaire

A pupil audit was given to children who were leaving the school. It contained five questions:

1. Please would you describe what it has been like being a pupil at West Kidlington School.

2. What have you enjoyed at the school?

3. What haven't you enjoyed at the school?

4. How could we improve our school?

5. Is there anything else you would like to say?

Here are some (anonymous) answers.

1. I have enjoyed being a pupil because there's a fair amount of work to do as well as having playtime. I also think that the work is normal so it's not to easy and not to hard. And the school is a nice environment to be in as well as having nice teachers.

2. I've enjoyed having quiet areas to sit down in and apparatus to play on. And I've enjoyed doing assemblies and learning about different values every month and hearing about different religions.

3. I haven't not enjoyed anything at the school only that I wish school could end later than 3.15 because I really enjoy learning about things and I also get to be with my friends.

4. I don't think it could be improved any more than what it is, but it would be nice to have a few more activities and apparatus to play on. And it would also be nice if we could use the school equipment at play time.

5. I think the school is a great school and I will be sad when I leave the school because everybody is nice and so are the teachers and its going to be very different leaving it.

And here is another set of answers.

1. Interesting and fascinating because we teach the usual subjects as well as a special extra – values. I can't remember being bullied, ever, or being made fun of, and that's what makes this school special.

2. I have really enjoyed talking to visitors, and being in the school council. I also liked going on school trips.

3. (no answer)

4. Have some tennis courts set a side for people playing tennis because they are more or less covering the play-ground, so that people that aren't playing tennis are not forced on to the field or into a corner of the play ground.

5. I would recommend this school to anyone because it has a warm feeling and as well as teaching values it has values.

This child wrote the word *values* in almost all his answers.

1. It has been a pleasure being at this school because the values make everyone polite and kind.

2. I have enjoyed all the values work and a kind environment.

3. I did get bullied a bit but my teacher sorted him out.

4. I don't think this school can be improved because the value work makes it whole.

5. I think values has upgraded the school 100 per cent!

Other children said, 'It's been brilliant, some of the best years ever'; 'It has been a really enjoyable time'; 'It has been very educating and fun to be a pupil at West Kidlington School'; and touchingly, 'I would recommend this school to people old and young, black and white. I have enjoyed helping teachers I have enjoyed learning about history. I liked being in Mrs Brands class because we used to sing weird songs.

From the 20 children in this sample there were few negative criticisms. Several had not been enamoured of maths – although of those, one or two said they were coming to grips with it. Many mentioned a wish for access at break times to the pond area (the problem is that the pond has to be supervised and there aren't enough staff to do it) and more play equipment (that old devil, finance). The large majority spoke of having a wonderful time and good friends, several mentioned how much they had enjoyed learning about values. A tiny and perhaps amazing minority agreed with the child who wanted school to go on longer in the afternoon so he could work longer. One said, 'We could improve the school by making playtimes shorter and learning more education at school.'

Year Five questionnaire

Linda Heppenstall's class, Year Five, had a similar questionnaire at the end of their school year. It had more questions in it. Question 3 was: What has learning about values taught you? Among the answers were:

'To put other people before yourself and to care about other peoples feelings.'

'To get on with my friends more. To realize trust is important.'

'How to behave properly, to get more friends, to wear a smile.'

'How to be a better person.' [This one came up frequently.]

'To be nicer to others, to relax, to not upset anyone and things like that.'

'It has taught me something about what we would do if we get upset and break friendship to just say sorry.'

'To be loving, caring and kind.' [Another favourite.]

'Learning about values has taught me that if your a nice person people are nice to you.'

Life after West Kidlington Primary School

The question is often asked, what happens when the children leave the rarefied environment of West Kidlington Primary School? (It generally carries the unspoken sub-text, *that's all very well in the safe, kind, protected gold bubble of a primary school but what about the **real** world?*) The rest of the world is not run along such egalitarian and defined lines; the rules are different and less clear, life at many secondary schools is much less peaceful. Neil Hawkes hopes the children's time at the school provides the strong foundation for making decisions and acting properly so that when they come up against sticky situations they won't just duck out. He is the first to acknowledge that teen years are difficult and teenagers naturally temperamental, and that the academic and social demands made upon them are more trying in the context of their physical maturing.

A research project undertaken to determine whether values teaching improves schools put eight questions to twelve-year-olds who had left the school a year earlier. Among them, it asked: What did learning about values teach you? A randomly chosen answer sheet said, 'to respect other people even the people I don't get on with and to treat people the way I would want to be treated.'

Q do you find you behave differently since learning about values?

A Yes it has taught me to be thoughtful towards others.

Q Did learning about values make you think differently about yourself and other people?

A Yes it did make me more close to all my friends especially my best ones and it encouraged me to work harder in some subjects.

Q Do you think that your school work improved because you learned about values?

A It had pushed me to do more and I did get good marks on pieces of work that I found difficult.

Q Has your behaviour changed since learning about values?

A I don't argue so much with people now.

The next question might be considered a leading one.

Q Do you think children in all schools should learn about values?

A Yes because it is important and it changes the way you look at things and your attitude.

Here is the teenager Alex Williams, author of the honesty rap (see Chapter Two). He left to go to a strongly academic, traditional, private school where he is treated more formally than he was at West Kidlington or would be at a state comprehensive. Alex is almost certainly treated more politely than he would be at many state secondary schools but there are subtle changes in the underlying ethos. He notices contrasts between the social life of the new school and that of the old one.

'When I was at West Kidlington I had two friends who went to different schools and – this might not sound very good – I don't think they were as thoughtful as we were. They weren't as considerate for their friends. They'd sometimes ring up and say, "Meet you at the park in ten minutes!" and then someone else would turn up and they'd go off with them and not bother to let you know.

'Now I'm at my new school I notice some people seem to deliberately make themselves hard to get on with. I don't know if they've got family problems. [A typical West Kidlington schoolchild's response to unpleasant behaviour is to assume that something is not going quite right in that child's life. It has been carefully taught.] No matter what happens, though, I've never lashed out. I usually do the West Kidlington thing and walk away. I notice the atmosphere's not quite as friendly. If you say, "Can we talk this over", somebody's just going to laugh at you. It can be uncomfortable, difficult to get on with people without them laughing. In the playground for example they might just throw your tennis ball away when you're playing against the wall – they'll just catch your ball and throw it over to the other side. Actually, they'd do things like that at West Kidlington too but they wouldn't throw it away, they'd catch the ball and then just drop it.

'At West Kidlington the teachers are much friendlier – you could really go up to them and tell them your problems, but probably that's a bit because you only have one teacher. Where I am now some of the teachers are fairly easy to talk to, but not many. At West Kidlington, you talk and they listen. Where I am now, they *sort of* listen – but I don't feel they really know you well enough to advise you. There aren't many women teachers. Women tend to be easier to approach; one in particular at my new school is incredibly approachable. A few of the male teachers are, but not to the same extent.

'The amount of respect is different. You can fairly easily get on with teachers now, and you can sometimes respect other pupils, but in general there's not as much as I was used to. We all did treat each other with real respect at my primary school.'

THE KIDLINGTON BLUEPRINT

Opening a conversation in which your children can tell their troubles and their fears, and also share their triumphs and fun, without being teased, laughed at, cut off, or any of the widely practised adult conversation-stoppers, is a finely tuned task. Talking after all isn't just making words come out of the mouth, but exchanging meaning, information, emotion.

How many adults say that in childhood they couldn't talk to their parents about things that seriously troubled them? Indeed, how many adults say that in childhood they couldn't talk to their parents about anything at all? Children soon find which bits of their lives to edit out, and then clam up on them. This inevitably creates distance, and it can leave terrible emotional scars.

There may be exciting things to talk about or there may be sad ones; whatever the subject, make time to talk. At the same time, make clear where you stand on moral questions. On the values teaching video that Neil Hawkes took with him to Mauritius, Year Five pupil Patrick, aged ten, said, 'Before I came here [to West Kidlington Primary School] I used to lie all the time and now I hardly ever lie. The one major thing I lied about, I owned up to it in the end. I accidentally broke a window and they asked who did it and I said it wasn't me, but then after a month I owned up.

'The reason I used to lie was I was scared of being told off, but now I know Mum and Dad will just talk to me and it will be sorted out. I'm very different from what I used to be.' *Just talk to me and it will be sorted out!* A clarion call. Now that Patrick trusts his parents he has no need of subterfuge.

Listening and talking lovingly and comprehendingly are as important as good food, a roof over their heads, protection from the elements, cuddles and maintenance of health. Notice whether you can open a topic out or whether unwittingly you close it down. Let them speak about their lives, while still making clear where you stand on moral questions. Try not to pigeonhole them into what you see as their main characteristic: the joker, the clever one, and so on. Then they will have a good deal to say to you.

CHAPTER 7

Parents Talking

PARENTS SEND THEIR CHILDREN TO WEST KIDLINGTON PRIMARY SCHOOL for a variety of reasons of which simple geography is high on the list. In Great Britain you have to live within a certain radius of a state school to be guaranteed a place there for your child. Thus the school draws many if not most of its children from the nearby housing estate, where long roads and neat crescents are lined with 1930s detached and semi-detached houses. However, the school has such a fine reputation that some parents have moved to the village of Kidlington just so that their children can attend it. This is true of Maz Yaqooeb, for whose family the move was entirely worthwhile. She says her two boys are much happier now, and she remarks that the elder one likes what he calls 'the strictness'.

For the Yaqooebs, the benefits for their children from the positive values programme was the critical factor in their choice. With no prior knowledge of the programme the Killicks believed that those offered to their son Stephen by the school's supportive environment would be the best one for him. They now regard the positive values emphasis very highly and take care to back it up at home.

Other parents also respond to the calm atmosphere and the happy, purposeful school community without necessarily knowing how this fine result is achieved. Few of them mention academic considerations first, although they naturally find the school's excellent record reassuring. For most of the parents, the fact that the children are balanced and untroubled is the most important consideration. From their first visit, parents like the way the children are: bright in outlook, polite and outgoing. This impression is strengthened by further acquaintance.

Many parents are happy to talk about the school. The following is a tiny, random selection, which shows remarkable concurrence on what is important.

Karen Clack

The first is Karen Clack, mother of Lizzie (eleven) and James (six). Everyone agrees that Lizzie and her mother are particularly close. Lizzie speaks well about values and her life in the previous chapter. She also mentions her huge family of teddies and stuffed toys, all of which have to be put to bed every night. Karen Clack thinks that Lizzie is extraordinarily grown-up in many ways and attributes it to the school, but she is also glad that Lizzie can go on being a child at least some of the time. Karen Clack assists in James's class once a week.

Karen Clack I help at the school, and I must say I'm very impressed by the teachers. You can't believe they've got so much control over the children. I don't say control that's in any sense unpleasant, it just means the children know what to do, they know what's expected. The children are all valued, that's the point, they're all made to feel important, so they're happy to comply with whatever is wanted.

Elizabeth has been very happy there and I know she'll be sorry to leave. You want them to be well educated, obviously, but you want them to be happy. The main thing about the school is the children *want* to go there. You never get them saying they've got a tummy ache or looking miserable about Monday morning, they really want to go and they really want to learn.

Elizabeth's very confident – far more than I or her father were at her age. I believe the reason for it is that they are valued. All the children are valued. If they've got a point to make, even if it's off the subject, they make it and are thanked and then the teacher will bring the conversation back without making them feel they've said something silly. That's wonderful. I can remember at school being frightened to put my hand up.

My son James is in Year Two, and we were worried about him to begin with. He's an introverted little boy and he's always a bit clingy. To be truthful he didn't like the nursery at the beginning, I think he was shy of adults. He came back home and said, 'boys don't work, boys play!' The nursery's very much centred on play [structured play, designed to teach] but they do a few learning things [perhaps more obviously educational to James] and he didn't like those parts of his day. But now that he's started school properly, he loves it! All over half-term he's been doing maths at home because he's enjoying it so much. If there's something they like at school they'll bring it home and do it here, they don't want to stop. The thing is, he feels confident now. There's an element of competitiveness with the boys, I don't think that's anything to do with the school, I think it's just because they're boys.

The parents find out about the values in different ways. The newsletters speak about them first and then of course when you go into the school and help like I do you see the value for the month up on the wall. I remember I thought it was a very good idea. It echoed what we were trying to do at home, it's very much part of how we wanted to bring them up ourselves anyway. Sometimes Elizabeth would say what the class assembly would focus on and then when you help there you see that it's not just in the assembly, it's carried on throughout the day. If a child is having some behaviour thing explained, maybe something at playtime, you see that the values are used then. [Children are not told off for inappropriate behaviour but the consequences of their action are pointed out. A clear distinction is made between the child and the action, in order to leave the child's self-respect intact.]

Actually, the best thing I can say about the values work is just how the school is when you go in there, the general day-to-day life. The children are quiet, they're busy, they're getting on with things – and they're enjoying themselves. When you walk in there's a lovely atmosphere and it's throughout the school. The children's work makes the school look good. The pride that's taken in the children's work is lovely, *all* their work gets put up. James and his class had to draw their mums, all the children had to draw mum and you should have seen some of them, they were really wild! They were lovely!

At the end of the day the best thing is making each child feel important and giving them a good education, and that's what they do.

Val Jordan

Val Jordan served for eleven years on the PTA while her two girls and one boy were attending the school. Her thirteen-year-old son Colin attended during the introduction of the values programme and is now at secondary school. He settled into his new school quickly and goes there cheerfully every morning.

Val Jordan Just as the passage between primary and secondary school was made easy by the partnership arrangements between the feeder schools and the new school, so the passage for Colin between the West Kidlington nursery and primary were easy too. It was more or less chance that sent our children there, because we were in the catchment area. But I've got quite involved. I think as a parent you should get involved, don't you, it's no good complaining if things aren't as you'd like them if you aren't prepared to do anything about it.

The thing I notice about Colin, which is perhaps unusual in a boy, is that he's more able to talk about his feelings than our girls are (they didn't go through the values programme as they are older). Sometimes he can grasp things that are very difficult, for example bad behaviour. You might see something when you're out that you don't like and you might say, 'they shouldn't have done that!' and Colin will say, 'Ah, but you see, their feelings were hurt, that's why they did it.' He pulls you up short quite often. For a thirteen-year-old boy he's quite mature at times.

For all that he's mature, he is still a thirteen-year-old boy – but one who has been taught to think things through and take responsibility for what he does. The way he sees life is not as a question of how much you can get away with but of what *should* be done. He's learnt that you don't think something isn't wrong just because it isn't noticed. The outlook he's got means that you hold a mirror up to yourself all the time.

The values programme isn't all that noticeable in specifics although it can make their behaviour vary, you notice something really basic like them being particularly helpful – especially at the start of the month! They might tidy up without being asked to, things like that. Mind you, they'll expect you to say thank you for it when they do something. Which is fair, after all.

Colin used to like the assemblies and he liked the fact that he knew exactly what was expected of him. He thinks about things. If he's got a problem he just goes away and he'll try to sort things out in his own mind. That's something they were told from the very beginning in the nursery school, 'Go away and have a little think about that.' The teachers said that to the children instead of just feeding them the answers and he liked it very much. Moving on from play school they all had their own little space, as well they had good routines such as listening to a story quietly instead of just fidgeting.

Put together it made a nice, friendly atmosphere and a very secure one because everybody knows the correct way to behave. I never get the impression that there's pressure put on them to do things, instead their capabilities are drawn out of them. Some schools just aim towards exams all the time, don't they? At West Kidlington they do the exams, but it isn't made out to be the be-all and end-all.

The best thing for Colin has been the security. It gave him confidence, and confidence all round in everything he does, but especially in school work. Children who've been to West Kidlington, if they can't grasp something immediately they're confident enough that they'll get it eventually, so they don't just drop at the first hurdle. It makes them more determined. It would be lovely if there was a similar regime at secondary school, wouldn't it? That would be marvellous!

Sharon Williams

The next parent has two children at the school, a boy and a girl, and she and her husband took some time deciding where to send them. Having assisted some of the teachers she has become so involved with life in the classroom that she is planning to do a teacher training course herself. The family live not far along the same road as West Kidlington School, on the way to Banbury.

Sharon Williams I chose the school very carefully, I looked at other possibilities as well. Apart from the choice of having children, I think the choice of school is the most important one you make. I'll admit I'm a bit afraid of secondary school. I don't think the emphasis is on caring and I disagree with people who say, 'they're older, they can look after themselves,' I think children still need assistance. They need first of all to be listened to, and then they need an example to follow that it's good to care about people. At West Kidlington it's very clear people care about you. I work there as a First Aider and I see how the older children care about the younger ones and about each other – they'll immediately go to a child in distress and they always help the younger children. That's true of all of them, not just one or two.

Apart from the fact that they're getting an excellent education, they're becoming good people. They're being shown that it's right to be thoughtful. It's the humanity of the place that's so good. They're well rounded, the children, and they're individuals. The school are doing what I do at home. I teach that *everything* you do is important. Anyone can do a nice little thing occasionally, but I think children need to know that everything they do is important.

The main point about the values thing is that it's freeing. My son loves feeling as if he's making a difference. He stands tall! He feels it's a benefit to him. If there's arguments going on, for example in the playground, he'll go and talk to the children and be the diplomat and he likes that, he feels he's done something good. That's the strength of the school, the children learn how to talk. Of course, everybody knows how to make words come out of their mouth but *their* words, the children's words, make a difference. They're given language and vocabulary – but also the feeling inside that it's OK to talk about difficult things, about things of their own particular concern. I think there are several reasons for this, the class teachers are marvellous at enabling them to talk, and then there's the School Council where the children really get talking about the running of the school.

Assemblies are another factor: I absolutely love them! They're so different! I always feel really peaceful, I feel warm, both during them and afterwards. The children come into them focused and thoughtful, and also getting ready to think. They're not quiet because they're being told off, they come in to get the most out of it. They know something special's going to happen.

I am aware for my own children that whatever they're doing at school, they're having a lot of fun. They really love going to school because it's enjoyable. They sit quietly during lessons, they work hard – they have lots of chances to have fun as they're learning. The thing is, they're appreciated, they're not being taught *at*. They do feel they're contributing. That's important: they know they can contribute as part of the whole lesson, and they know they're valued. They tell me the fun things they've been doing and they may be in subjects they haven't been particularly successful at. Josh had a super games lesson recently, and he's not at all a games person. He was terribly pleased about it. The teachers are very good with him, they've thought about getting him to take part in his own way.

I think the values could work in secondary schools but really if you were to ask me, I would love my children to stay at West Kidlington until they're sixteen years old – even eighteen years old! If you knew the number of parents who say that! They know their children are safe, secure and happy there. It's got to be that the teachers are different, because the children aren't different. When I was at secondary school it was just a question of churning out factory fodder. I'm not saying it was the teachers' fault, I think it was how it was seen.

With children it's self-discipline that counts but at secondary schools I don't think they trust the children to make the right decisions, they're not given enough trust. I think children are just numbers at secondary school. The children at West Kidlington are shown they are trusted and I believe if you're taught it enough it becomes part of your psyche. They know the standard.

I want my children to grow, but I want them to be disciplined within a loving framework – not punishment, but love and understanding. I think it's very hard in education at the moment. I think it's one of the most underrated jobs there is. I want to come in to it because I absolutely love being with children. When you see the light coming on in their eyes because they've understood something – that's the best thing there is.

Often the work they've done in assembly teaches me, the value of the month especially. The children tell me what they've learnt, but the whole experience is teaching me an appreciation of them. As much as we love them, I don't think we give children the credit they deserve for their deep thought. They have a freshness, a way of looking at something, that is wonderful. Take humility, which is the word they've been doing recently. To me it means not being boastful but my son came home talking about doing things for other people. It was a different concept from mine and it was drawn into caring about others – he was thinking of it in relation to how it would affect people.

I think the first thing they learn is to value themselves – realising you are a good person. Without valuing yourself, how can you value other people? These are fundamentals they're learning and I am very pleased about it. They respect themselves because they respect others. You must have a positive feeling about who you are in the world before you can truly give. You can see it in the way they talk to each other as equals, across the age ranges, the very small children too. And they always listen. I find that really important, that they listen to each other. A lot of that is because of the example of the teachers, and because they have reflective time in the classroom.

There's going to be a lot of really nice people around in a few years' time, because what you learn before you're seven or eight – or even eleven – certainly stays with you. That's the building blocks, the foundation of the sort of person you are. I believe my children have the capacity to find their own answers to the difficult questions. They have intelligence and the reasoning ability, they're articulate, they can do it. And that's because of the wonderful start they're having now.

Claire Killick

The Killicks were so keen on West Kidlington School when their son Stephen (now nine) was due to go to nursery school that they were considering moving house to get him a place there. Fortunately, he got one of the places allocated randomly to children who live slightly outside the catchment area. The family home is about four miles away and Stephen goes to school by bus.

Claire Killick We chose the school because Stephen was very shy and had no confidence and I'd heard West Kidlington had an excellent reputation. I'd heard there was no bullying, and that's quite rare these days, isn't it? I'd heard about the values taught, and the old-fashioned ways, we were desperate to get him in. We'd heard of the partnership with parents and that sounded good as well. I think they want the best for the child, for the individual. Everything is geared to the ability of the individual.

You can go and see them at any time. We've been to see Mr Hawkes not long ago because of questions over Stephen's progress. He was very open with us, very friendly. He said, 'What's *your* opinion, what do *you* think?' There's a feeling that they want to listen to you. The problem with Stephen has been that his confidence has been low in class. He's very shy, but now he will put his hand up, he's been given extra help and he feels valued at school. Before, he was absolutely terrified.

Mr Hawkes said we needed to think about how to help him get from his mind to his hand, or maybe from his brain to a practical outcome. He gave us some pointers how we can make him more independent at home, for example he said we might make sure that Stephen gets his own schoolbag ready, gets himself out at 8.35am, and that we might try not to talk for him when he's shy, but let him get there by himself. It's true I do step in where sometimes I shouldn't, but Mr Hawkes understood that. He didn't say it was going to be easy. He also said how Stephen was at school – happy!

All the staff genuinely care and what strikes you as a parent is that you're welcome at any time. I'll pop into the classroom to see his teacher any day before or after school and they're quite willing to talk to me. To help Stephen, they suggested that I might go in and help so that he could see me around for some of the time. Even if I'm not working with him I'm usually in the same room, just to be there for his confidence. I must say I found it an eye-opener. I go in Friday mornings. It's all so calm, so well-behaved. Mrs Bryden, for example, if she wants silence she'll just hold up her fingers like this [both hands in the air, first fingers slightly extended] and say, 'It's my turn to speak now, children' – and there's instant silence! You can't believe it until you see it. It isn't that the children don't get excited: they get very excited about some things. They get excited about their class assembly, they love it, all the getting ready and learning their words. In the hallway the atmosphere is warm and there's always a lovely welcome. Children all say 'hello', they don't just file past. I remember my first visit there, it felt warm and welcoming.

Stephen now produces work on time where before he used to panic. He really cares about it. He's absolutely animated! He comes home, he says, 'Can we do that at home now Mum?' That's the thing about the school, the children actually want to be there. The first couple of years Stephen was fearful but now he can't wait to go. To begin with the teachers had concerns. He wasn't finishing pieces of work they gave him, he'd start off with the others and then give up half way. We were called in and they asked me, 'What do you do to get him to do things?' I said, take away something, a special thing or an extra. They said, 'Can we?' and I said yes. They tried one or two things but the one that worked was to send work home if it wasn't finished during class. He doesn't get told off, it's just, 'Oh, Stephen, if you don't get that done will you just take it home?' He always does get it done now, because he doesn't want to have to bring it home. Well, almost always!

The thing is, they make you feel part of a relationship, which is very constructive. I was anxious. I always thought: 'Must get it right!' – and they taught me not to think like that. They made me at ease, they really helped me. They said, 'Calm down!' I think it's sometimes hard work but it's very satisfying, very rewarding to make more effort. It's important to do it, things like tables, reading and spellings. You have to remind yourself to talk about the values. I say, 'What's your value at the moment then, son?' He'll say 'trust', or 'caring', or whatever, and I make a point of discussing it. I've enjoyed working with the school to help them. They've made me calmer; told me I was doing a good job. We always wanted to be part of his education and we feel valued as parents – they don't just take over, they say your opinion really matters. They care about what you're saying.

What do I like best about it? I couldn't say one thing, I like the whole concept. It's friendly, they look after you, and not just the children but the parents too. They set a standard of learning, they look for good behaviour that's achievable, you're treated as a human being, they've got time for everybody, the children are taught to care. It's an all-round lovely school. The staff are smashing, the office is great. I've never heard anybody who had a bad word for them.

In a sentence? It gives the children a value on themselves.

Maz Yaqooeb

Among the most motivated of all West Kidlington parents, the Yaqooeb family moved house so the children could get into the school. Mrs Yaqooeb was born and brought up in Sheffield, south Yorkshire. She is a university graduate and mother of three boys. She believes that bringing her children to the school has transformed them.

Maz Yaqooeb We moved our children here [from a school in an insalubrious suburb a couple of miles away] and they're much happier. They're thriving. I like the discipline, there are clear lines. My elder boy wasn't doing well at his other school, he stayed two years and it didn't get any better. At first you think they'll get used to it but he didn't and we had to take him away. He came home from this school in his first week and said, 'Mum, they're strict but they're fair!' – and it got me right in the heart. He likes what he calls the strictness, it means he knows where he is, and he recognises that it makes things easier all round. As a parent, the difference you notice straight away is that the teachers listen to you! Most other places they just brush you aside, you get the impression they'd rather be doing something else, but here you get their full attention.

My elder boy, Wassim, is interested in computers. From day one that's all he wanted to do, so that's how they got him to read, so he can find out more about computers. They did it and he reads all the time now – but only about computers. These days I think you've got to take part in everything a lot more and not trust the government to do it for you. My parents' generation trusted the government, trusted the people in charge, but we don't, we've been let down too often. I read with my children and I hope to help in the school when the youngest is old enough to be there all day. I'd like to give something back. With a school like this that's doing so much good work, you want to help, don't you?

Nicola Groves

Nicola Groves has a family association with West Kidlington Primary School that spans three generations. Her grandfather was a governor from the school's foundation in 1956 until 1997, she was a pupil and now her son Joseph attends. This is the sort of pedigree more to be expected at a traditional public school than a state primary in a provincial suburb and is therefore rather surprising. It puts Nicola in a position to make historic comparisons. She speaks of continuity of quality, if not of style. She says the big difference is that 'it seems like a child's school now'.

Nicola Groves I'm very positive about Joseph coming here. The atmosphere is very good, the children are calm and well-behaved. More than anything else, they're taught how to be nice to people. They're taught respect for one another and I believe that's very rare these days. I came here in 1978 when Paul Canterbury was the head and I only have good memories. Mr Canterbury wasn't frightening like headmasters used to be, he was very kind and caring towards everybody. That was how everybody was, even the kitchen staff were always pleasant.

Joseph went to a Montessori nursery in Kidlington but he was always going to come here, there was never any thought of anywhere else. I worried a bit about the size of this school but they deal with it well. I think he's found his feet. I like the layout of his classroom, it's nice when you go in, the work on the walls is very nice. Joseph's happy. He especially likes his friends, playing in the sand, and his teacher.

I can remember good times when I was here. It was a very close, safe, secure environment. I get the impression it's a real community, and I like that idea. You sense a strong community spirit, with the children and the parents very involved. I also think it's significant that they hold on to their staff for so long.

Janice Bridges

The correspondent for the school governors, Janice Bridges, is the mother of two children who attended West Kidlington throughout their primary schooldays. Her involvement goes back ten years and her enthusiasm for the school is great. She still teaches cycling proficiency there.

Janice Bridges My children are positive about themselves, self-confident, they have a good sense of humour. West Kidlington was a very major part of their lives and both of them talk about it with great fondness. I was very happy with the children coming through the school and when I was asked to work here I was so pleased.

They've carried on the values at their new school, all the things they've learned here, their behaviour's the same now as it was then. Nothing can really throw them. If something happens they just handle it. They understand that everyone's different. My son had difficulty at the new school with one child who got aggressive with him, pushing and shoving, that sort of thing. He came home and told me about it but what was striking was that he said, 'Of course we must consider the fact that he's got problems.' He will try and understand the other person's point of view, what's making them say or do things. He's very aware of things around him and he's a good communicator.

I like the way the children talk who've been at this school. They've always been keen to talk to adults and that means they communicate very well with teachers. My sons will ask about their concerns, they'll say what's bothering them. At parents' evenings more or less all of the teachers at their new school comment on it, they say how easily they can talk to them. The boys have been encouraged to ask questions and taught how to do it, they're very polite. Another good thing about them is that they'll always apologise if anything goes wrong.

I was at a parents' evening recently at their new school. The secondary teachers said how polite my children were and they said it was delightful to have them. I can't help but think it was West Kidlington's influence. I'm so glad they came!

Ellen Gardner

The Gardner family live practically next door to the school so the decision to send their children there was taken on grounds of geography, although Ellen Gardner says she had heard from several of her nephews and nieces who were pupils there that it was a nice school. There are four children: Sam (eleven), Thomas (nine), Phoebe (seven) and Abby (five). Sam's views are included in the previous chapter.

Ellen Gardner I'm from Kidlington but I went to a different school and we were happy there, I enjoyed going to school. When you put your children's names down you don't know what they're going to get. You don't know anything about education or Ofsted or anything really, when you start. Sam started at the same time as Neil [Mr Hawkes] and the values thing happened in Year Two. Sam came home talking about assembly and he'd say what the word of the month was. He explained how they were told what it means and how we can do it ourselves. Like trust, for example. At home we always say, 'We expect you to tell the truth and if you don't you're not trusting us,' and the children understand that. Sam still talks about the assemblies, he says, 'Mr Hawkes plays lovely music, Mummy, and it's very soothing.' It's made him appreciate Mozart, which they play, and because of that, other classical composers.

We always have a discussion at tea-time as a family and we all say the best bits of our day, and the worst, and how we can improve tomorrow. Then Dad comes home and tells us what he's done in *his* day and it all starts again.

I'm on the PTA and I go in three mornings a week to help out.

I do most things, usually reading or helping the children finish a piece of work, but it could be almost anything. When you go in to help, the children are so polite. They always say, 'Thank you for coming in,' and the older ones ask, 'Is there anything I can do for you?' Last term I went to the Isle of Wight as a helper with nineteen children from Year Six. It was my first experience of taking a group away on a school holiday. There was just me and Bet [Mrs Brands] in a hotel with all the children, and they were extremely well-behaved. The hotel people kept praising us, they said they couldn't believe there were so many children there. They were so quiet, one of the hotel people said, 'Did you leave them all behind?' The manager said they were a credit to their teachers and their school. They said that before we arrived they'd been a bit nervous about us coming but then they kept on saying what a pleasure it was having us.

Sam has certainly gained in confidence from being there. He's always in the headmaster's office, must be several times a day! We tease him about it. We *never* went in the headmaster's office in my schooldays – and you *never* went in the staff room like they do at West Kidlington! Sam doesn't believe me when I tell him schools could be like that. He certainly has lots of confidence. The way he talks to adults – to his granny and older people – is very good. His granny says he's so grown-up for his age, and I think he's very mature for his eleven years. He's very good academically, he's quite clever and he is happy. If he's worried or upset he'll come and talk to me about it but it doesn't last long.

Sam can stand up in front of a whole school assembly and talk to everybody. I go to assemblies too if I'm invited, I enjoy them. It's amazing how they get that many kids in that hall and they're so quiet. I notice that no one drags their feet when they're walking in, they stand nice and straight, their heads high. No one slouches. I love their singing! It's a different way of silence the children have there – they do their silence out of respect.

So far I think Sam's got a jolly good education, and he's got that extra bit: he's brilliant with other people, adults as well as kids, he's got the gift of the gab. I get lots of people saying to me, 'Where do your children go to school?' and then when I tell them they say they've heard it's a nice school. Even people in Banbury [17 miles] or Warwickshire [30 miles] say so! The school motto carries a lot: *care and excellence.* The children are very caring, the teachers are very caring, and as far as I'm concerned, Alex [the caretaker] is very caring as well!

PC Colin Black

The fact that so many parents like to help at West Kidlington is lucky, because the school is under pressure to accept ever greater numbers of pupils, and the adult:child ratio would otherwise be much less favourable than it is. Police Constable Colin Black gives one of his days off every fortnight to assist with Years Two and Six. He has two daughters there, Kathryn (eight) and Heather (five).

Colin Black Kathryn loves the school, she's very settled – they both are. My wife and I looked round all the local primary schools before we made the decision to send Kathryn there. We spent an hour in each one and they were all reasonably good but the striking thing about West Kidlington was the atmosphere. From the moment we walked in we knew it was the one. Kathryn said so too, she came with us on all the visits.

The behaviour was a big part of it: it's first class. I go in every other Monday to help out, a bit of reading, a few sums, whatever takes some of the pressure away from the teachers. I think it's important to help out in these times of big classes; I feel I want to give a little bit back. It's easy as parents to drop them off at the school gate at nine o'clock and pick them up again at quarter past three but you need to do more than that, I think you need to take part more. It has to be a partnership to instil values. But I'd have to say it's good fun, the contact with the children, I enjoy it.

The value words are very good. All parents want a good education but the children need to be brought up good citizens as well. The way they do it at the school, it has more structure as opposed to just picking them [positive values] up. If they keep up as they've begun, these children will grow up good citizens who accept responsibility and show consideration.

I've seen some marvellous things there. On Sports Day there was a young disabled child taking part in one of the races. He really struggled, he was miles behind the rest of the field and they all cheered and cheered when he came in, all the children were genuinely pleased for him and he was so pleased himself, he could have been the winner. In some ways he *was* the winner.

I have to come back to the atmosphere. The calmness. It allows all the kids to prosper, there are no winners and losers, everybody is valued, and if they feel valued they give their best.

Andrew Jones

The Jones family consists of Andrew and Jan and three children, Sian (nine), Tao (seven) and Ebony (two). Sian and Tao attend the school. Tao is autistic and was mentioned in Chapter Five. He is included in all school activities, and staff and children make sensitive provision for his abilities and inabilities without ever making him feel different. Ebony will attend when she is old enough. Andrew and Jan had different impressions of the school at the beginning. Now Andrew's involvement is very great as he has taken on the voluntary job of parent governor.

Andrew Jones The parent governor is perceived as a critical friend and I see my role quite often as a sort of mediator. Parents might come to me and say they don't like this or that, or they're concerned about the way they're doing something at school. Recently it's been about literacy hour [the government-prescribed reading and writing session, interpreted slightly differently in different schools]. My own personal concern is with Tao. He's doing really well, he's continued to do really well and naturally I want it to go on, so I go to the teacher and say, 'how will literacy hour affect Tao?' They say, 'It won't, much', so I feel OK about it.

Quite a few parents are a bit intimidated by the professions. The teachers are quite a nice bunch at West Kidlington but as a parent you can have an easier relationship with other parents than you can with teachers, which is why the parents tell me things first. I don't often wait to bring things to the governors' meeting – I'll take it to the office or to the head teacher direct, and sort it out there and then. My main motives for being a governor were: 1. I really thought they'd done fantastically well with Tao, they were very supportive, and 2. Rather selfish, really: I wanted to make sure by being involved I would have a bit of influence.

When we first went round the school my wife Jan loved the quietness straight away but I was troubled by it. I thought, are they going to be like little androids? We went back there again and chatted to Mr Hawkes. He was very spiritual; you could see it. He told us that he wants a calm school, with clear and recognisable boundaries, which children need to make them feel safe. Very clear morals. I had an impression of spirituality, a real spiritual vibe.

Since then what I've found is there are brilliant teachers, brilliant LSAs [Learning Support Assistants] – especially Mrs Smith – and everyone really cares about the school and the community. You can talk to everyone, the dinner ladies, the breaktime helpers, Alex – and there's a real spirit of unity. To tell you the truth I didn't like Kidlington as a place all that much when I moved there but in the school there's a real feelgood factor, a real sense of harmony.

When Tao first started at West Kidlington we had quite a bit of anxiety and a great many meetings between us and the staff. I think there was an element of caution on both sides. The situation was new to us and new to them. We went to everyone for advice and we got conflicting advice and it caused tension initially. This has now completely evaporated and we're in a partnership. In one way, they were encouraging us to fight for our own rights. We were a pain in the backside! We were – and are – demanding. But the school don't want anything less for Tao than we do. He's made remarkable progress and he deserves credit and so do they.

I think it's a model for other schools and parents how to work together. The teachers' assistants have been brilliant. They showed an enormous amount of love – not out of charity, but real. Tao, like any other child, needs boundaries. His teachers have always communicated well with us and us with them, they have no qualms about saying, 'We're not sure about x' – for example Tao's play-fighting, mimicking Spider Man, etc. I encourage that at home but they said we need to make sure that Tao is very clear there are little ones at school and he must learn to make the distinction. They say things about homework, for example they'll tell us to spend less time on reading and maths and concentrate more on something else because it's what they're doing at school. There have even been times when they'll say at the end of the week, 'He's worked hard, let him off!'

Everyone deserves a pat on the back. I don't think he could have made the same level of progress at another school, to be quite honest with you.

THE KIDLINGTON BLUEPRINT

These West Kidlington parents did not discuss their interviews with each other, nor were they in the same room when they were given, but they were remarkably in agreement on the positive qualities of the school. What they see as the favourite elements are a fair summary of the Blueprint. And how they see the interpretation of the Blueprint is of critical importance. They like:

- the discipline – and the fact that it is loving and not oppressive.

- the hard work – and the fact that the children so clearly enjoy doing it.

- the building of thoughtful, considerate characters, demonstrated by the children's concern for each other and genuine joy in their classmates' successes.

- the way the children have been shown how to see each other's points of view and be sensitive to each other's moods.

- the children's confidence, both socially and with their work.

- the children's calmness and motivation.

More than once, the parents observed how much their children were teaching them. This is not such an unusual remark, but perhaps the quality of what the children teach is perceived more finely. 'I think sometimes we don't give them enough credit for their deep thought' is a most sensitive observation, and one which is prepared to be humble in the adult role.

All the parents like the definition of discipline as fairness and clarity, a loving framework in which the rules are kind and just. It rehabilitates a word that has had a rough time as a justification of or even a synonym for punishment.

The definition of positive values can easily include positively valuing each individual child, their aspirations and their quality. You can love and admire someone's ability to behave like a sensible, balanced, responsible, hard-working, grown-up eleven-year-old as well as loving them for their devotion to an extraordinary and to some minds excessive collection of stuffed toys.

CHAPTER 8

The Kidlington Blueprint

THE WORK AT WEST KIDLINGTON MAKES DEMANDS ON TEACHERS THAT are qualitatively different from demands made in most other schools. The main difference is in the level of honest self-appraisal needed to ensure that the adults participate with the children and don't simply impose their own worn-out agendas in the old worn-out way. This work makes the same demands on the parents as it does on the children. It is nothing less than trans-generational, joint effort, the same effort made from different starting-points. It is a shared adventure.

If the demands are great, the rewards are matchless. They consist in seeing that we have been instrumental in helping children to be happy, bright, balanced, respectful and honourable. The rewards consist in contributing to the lives of children who can take their proper places in the adult world, children who are the purposeful citizens of the future. Could there be anything more important for adults than joining in with our children's positive development? Joining in starts with good attitudes. From his 30 years' experience with children, Neil Hawkes offers the following thoughts.

Neil Hawkes Underlying this work is a belief that you don't do it *to* others. What we really do is invite people to explore notions of themselves and thus discover a path that leads to life being fulfilling. It is a question of enabling people to work from the inside out; it's something you do yourself, not something that is done *to* you. The whole philosophy lasts because it does that. Essentially, you are invited to take part in being on an inward journey, which affects you at a deep level. It would be terrible if parents had a list up in the house somewhere of things headed, THOU SHALL, because the moral discourse, the act of discussion, is crucial. The most important thing this work offers is the opportunity to talk to children about values and meaning and their practical impact in life. Through Socratic dialogue, through question and answer, change happens.

For children, learning about positive values takes more than, as some people think, somehow catching them by being in the vicinity of people who are living them. Values are indeed caught but we must provide children with the opportunity to catch them, and there is no real forum for it in society. We must hear, we must understand and we must implement these things in our lives. This implies that we need to be aware of our own prejudices that have come through from our backgrounds and our cultural context. When we consider the value words we must look as carefully as possible at them and not bias children because of our own limited understanding. Incidentally, this is an invaluable exercise for our own development

Between adult and child there must be an open, trusting relationship – but one in which the child knows the boundaries. Certainly they will spot inconsistency quickly, and hot air too! You mustn't pretend to be honest if you're not. You mustn't pretend to be anything you're not. None of us is perfect but we all have an opportunity to develop. Spiritually, we're all on that journey.

At the same time it's important to keep a balance with this work, it's important not to do too much soul-searching because that can so easily lead to a state of mind that says, 'I'm not good enough, let's leave it to someone else.' We all start from where we are. If we love our children we will want to enable them to feel they are in control of their own destiny and not on some sort of life conveyor belt which they cannot influence. People who are engaged in spiritual work are of all types and intellects. It's not dependent on how clever you are, indeed cleverness can be an impediment. Actually it's for all of us, grandparents as well. Grandparents are tremendously important to children's lives. When they are living close enough to take part they can be a wonderful influence.

Parents should be able to learn from children. We tend to

think adults have wisdom but in reality children can help us gain clarity of understanding in spiritual matters. Children often have extremely clear perceptions, which can all too easily be belittled or ignored. Adults don't realise that they close down conversations with children. I hear parents say things which somehow conclude the interchange when the child is still trying to find out something, or offer something. The parents don't know they're doing it, I don't believe it's deliberate.

You need to seek ways of developing a relationship to enable the child to trust you, not to just negatively respond. There is great subtlety in an adult making clear what is and is not acceptable but at the same time developing the trust that enables conversation; a feeling that you're allowed to make a mistake and it won't matter. Adults have to make clear, first and foremost, that we don't lie. This means that if you agree to do something you'll do it – even sanctions like them going to bed early for some reason. If a child knows where the boundaries are, and it's clear, the child isn't having to guess, 'If I say this, what will happen next?'

Next we need to develop patience. Almost limitless, this one. And the ability to listen. Never tell a child off, only the behaviour! You must always leave the strength and the selfhood of the child intact, they must never receive the impression that you don't love them. There again, it's not just in what you say, it's in how you behave. It's no good saying to a child, 'It's all right', and then demonstrating that you don't mean it.

It's important for parents and family to establish what the adults will and won't do. If you disapprove of smoking on principle, for example, and yet you smoke yourself, would you be able to tell a child not to do it? I disapprove of being rude to people who appear to be different, it's a form of prejudice. It follows that I must not, however subtly, alter my behaviour towards people who seem different in outlook or appearance or understanding.

Because as adults we are all so busy these days, many if not most children are really crying out for our attention. When we give it, this attention should not just be material. People try to buy off their guilt over their children by buying them things when what is needed is time for focused attention. It needn't be hours and hours but it needs to be available, and if possible available every day. Listening is the key: listen to them! I can see that may be a new exercise. Even in the classroom we can get tired of listening and unconsciously start to screen out certain things but somehow you have to stop yourself doing that.

There may be a qualitative difference between listening and hearing. Sometimes if you have the radio on in the corner of the room and are doing something else, you're vaguely hearing what's on the radio but you are not in any concentrated sense listening to it. The quality of listening to your children, listening not just to their words but to what is underlying their words, to what they are deeply saying to you, is vital to this work.

Begin as early as you can: it's very difficult to say to a fourteen-year-old, 'Let's talk!', when you've had no history of it. You then have to try and do all the building up of communication and trust that has been missed up to that point, and it will be a much more difficult task than if you'd worked it all out as you went along. letting your child give you advice is a way of showing that you value the child, and his or her opinions. I have often done this with my own children. At the moment my youngest, who has enormous common sense, is acting as a good brake on my thoughts and actions.

Storytelling is a most wonderful means of getting values into the day. Stories have always been used for investigating the way things work in the world, and the way we work with them. So are pictures. Storytelling is one of the ancient ways in which adults and children have interacted, given and received love, enjoyed each other's company. There are many books that can help you with this and no doubt you know some of them already. I heard a lovely story about a family of two parents and three teenage boys, all very close and good friends, a family with enormous love and respect for one another, and the father has always read to the boys at night and still does to the two younger ones. The eldest boy is eighteen and has left home and the youngest boys in the family are fifteen and twelve years old and might well have thought they were too grand to be read aloud to but apparently they don't. The book I heard about was *Lord of the Rings*. The reading was done upstairs in semi-darkness, so they were entirely concentrated on it. Apparently the boys loved it, it was a time of pure communication for them, imagination, pictures in the mind, and the total attention of their father.

When I heard this story it recalled another one, this time about a teacher in Germany who reads aloud to her class of fourteen-year-olds. She does it at the beginning of many of her English language classes and the pupils are not allowed to draw or doodle. They have to fold their arms on their desks, put their heads on their arms, close their eyes and *see* the story. Apparently some of them object to begin with because they think it is kids' stuff. Later they all say they love it: it opens up the vast and wonderful potential of imagination in their minds. Afterwards they have to tell the story themselves in English and at that point it becomes an academic exercise, but until then it's pure, creative imagination.

Helping children to develop their imagination is another vital part of the adult's task and there is in general not enough opportunity for it at the moment, everything is factual. Television and films are passive, you just watch them, you don't have to do any of the work yourself. To think about values you need imagination. It gives the ability to look at different possibilities in the future, and that's why stories are so important to very young children. If you can't imagine, you can't imagine how things will get better. When as a parent you are reading or telling stories to your children you can say, 'What do you think will happen next? The person in the story, what does she look like? How does she feel? What might she want to say?' Without stories you can't really understand other people or their behaviour and understanding of this kind is most important.

When you are out and about with your children, looking at the world through positive-tinted glasses, be sure to point out the good things that happen. This was suggested at the end of Chapter Two and it is another joyful thing to do. Maybe someone is specially helpful to someone in the supermarket, or a child is behaving particularly well. You can say something about it and treasure the moment. We can provide the antidote to the habit of looking for things to criticise by looking for things to praise.

An important quality for all parents to develop is that of respect. When I watch parents it is clear that the ones with the most successful relationships are the ones with respect. The children are not being treated as a product when proper respect is there. This implies respect for yourself, too. I have tremendous respect for anybody who is helping a child to develop at the beginning of the twenty-first century, the job is made so difficult by the many influences they'll come under, so many of them negative ones. And parents are often having to do the job in near-isolation now that the extended family or any real community are so rarely available.

It is important to believe in what you are doing. If the world is going to be a tolerable place to live, everyone has to seriously consider the big questions. I believe that otherwise the social degeneration will be horrendous. I will put it as strongly as this: we either come to grips with the big ethical problems, face up to the big and dangerous compromises, or we have a chance, even a strong probability, of civilisation disintegrating.

This is not a handbook; we are simply offering ways that we have found to be successful in this most vital task, ways that may be worth thinking about. The Kidlington Blueprint suggests ideas of using our happy, successful, school experience as a map you could use to get to your chosen destination. We could always do more, we can continue to do more. Above all forgive your children when things go wrong, and forgive yourself too, and have the determination to get up and try again.

The quality I would most like to give to children is determination. The children who develop wonderfully, the children who really flower, are those with determination to look at themselves and change and then persevere still more. And what's true for them is true for adults too.'

Values for adults as much as for children

The generations have so much in common that it was easy for Neil Hawkes to list the needs of adults and children. Here it is:

- To be loved.

- To be valued as people.

- Security.

- To know what is expected of them.

- Balanced experiences, e.g. active/quiet, sound/silence, communication/reflection, taught skills/exploratory work.

- Help in developing their own web of relationships.

- Self-awareness and knowledge of the world outside.

- Creative experiences including external exploration and internal reflection.

- Full involvement in the process of education.

Something for adults to consider are the six aspirations for West Kidlington teachers:

- Consistency

- Kindness

- Fair dealing

- Strength

- Truthfulness

- Trustworthiness.

And Neil Hawkes' observations can be put into simpler form.

WHO YOU ARE (qualities to aspire to)	WHAT YOU DO (behaviour to aspire to)
Consistent	Listen, and hear
Self-appraising	Join in with the children's effort
Honest	Have an open relationship
Aware of your prejudices	More action than soul-searching
Humble	Include extended family
Open	Be ready for questioning
Respectful	Be able to learn yourself
Giving	Give time
Determined	Notice positive things
Loving	Help to develop imagination

Change and self-observation are constant factors. This does not mean the unproductive, beating yourself up kind of observation but simply noticing habits of thinking, left-over attitudes. Often you will find that you can let go of automatic, negative responses. 'Oh, that will never work!' 'It's your fault!' or the miserable and habitual, 'It's *my* fault!' Practise taking the word fault out of your vocabulary and substitute in your mind, 'responsibility'. It is much more positive. Something needs to be put right, and I could be the one to do it.

Talking about responsibility

John Heppenstall once led his class of nine- and ten-year-olds in a half-hour discussion on shared responsibility because the previous evening when he asked a child to pick up a piece of litter the child truthfully replied, 'But I didn't drop it!' John Heppenstall said, 'Maybe not, but we all like to see a tidy classroom, I'm tidying up, and you could be the one to pick up that bit of paper.' The class talked about what action is right for the good of the community, when to stick on the personal responsibility principle and when to let it go for the sake of general harmony. How much do I do simply for myself, and how much do I do because it helps the whole? Where do I end and where do you begin? A question that recurs all through life, and an illustration of how an apparently small incident can lead to a useful and productive consideration of larger questions.

All sides of the dilemma were aired in a thorough discussion. There is, of course, no single solution but the children were given the means to see it from different angles and to see that although no single answer is automatically right several may be appropriate. This sort of impromptu exercise is one they often do at the school. It uses the children's mental faculties as well as their moral and spiritual ones, it is interesting and it engages their minds. Any situation can be used for similar objective consideration, and of course, for using the positive value words.

Talking is crucial. We all talk, but focused, concentrated talk that listens to the other person's point of view, not simply waiting for them to stop so that we can get our own next remark in, but giving real attention – that sort of communication is quite rare. Let's compare real talk with the *second* viewing of a film. The first time you see a film you remember the plot, the pictures and some of the dialogue. That is like ordinary talk. On the second viewing you notice shifts of mood, subtler messages. We could try to pay attention to children talking at the level of the second film viewing.

We already know our own children (of course) but if we listen to them more carefully we may notice that they bring us different thoughts, fresh observations, different worries and triumphs from the last time we saw them. We may notice that this time they are responding differently to a situation, perhaps more positively, perhaps less. We may notice what is behind their words. Every single moment, every interchange, is slightly and subtly different.

Positive values at home

Several of the parents in the last chapter mentioned how much they have enjoyed observations their children have made when they have come home from school. Parents especially enjoyed being caught out by their children. 'He made me think differently!' they said, or, 'My son said, "You can see why that person does that, it's because they are unhappy" – and he made me understand it better.' When Val Jordan said of her son Colin, 'He pulls me up short quite often,' she said it with surprise and approval. When Sharon Williams said, 'As much as we love them I don't think we give children the credit they deserve for their deep thought,' she made a profound observation. Children can teach us as much as we can teach them. Talking about value and meaning deepen understanding and the gains are on both sides of the conversation, both sides of the age divide. Here is the great joy of it: both parties will learn something as long as they listen, and enjoy themselves.

Comprehension of abstract principles is a refinement not reached by children until they are about eleven, so always use practical examples in moral discourse. And take the lead. Neil Hawkes says, 'we're in a culture that thinks someone else will fix it, and this delegation of responsibility for bringing up children must be given back. Parents can't delegate it any longer. Because values are not in the consciousness, because they are not part of the everyday conscious mind, parents have abdicated responsibility and the vacuum has been filled by television and popular culture. But children are more likely to pick up mixed messages from television; there's no central guiding principle to television morality beyond what sells.

'Values education doesn't happen naturally, you have to make it happen. Parents may not be aware that something needs to be done. Once they have taken that in, they need to determine in their own mind what's important. If they don't, they leave a vacuum to be filled by negative, materialistic messages. In terms of being an example you have to start from day one and before. Help the child to be strong! You also need to make a child aware of negative values as well as positive ones, and what they can cause.'

Once adults have got their heads round the ideas of change, self-observation and parity of effort, the next element is *good solutions*. This naturally returns to the positive value words. They are endlessly useful. For those with an interest in the Bible it may be worth noting that the first ten commandments given to the Children of Israel before they uncomprehendingly made the golden calf (money) to worship – were all positive. Peace and Love and Trust, for example. These commandments were before Thou Shalt Not, which is anyway not quite an accurate translation from the Hebrew. The correct translation is, 'a proper man would not,' a very different emphasis. So now we are returning to the original idea of the positive, with the expectation of proper outcomes from understanding.

quality	*co-operation*
unity	*understanding*
peace	*honesty*
happiness	*appreciation*
hope	*courage*
patience	*love*
caring	*friendship*
humility	*thoughtfulness*
simplicity	*tolerance*
trust	*responsibility*
freedom	*respect*

All the teachers at West Kidlington School were asked to consider the words and make suggestions for using them at home. They contributed them at different lengths and in different styles. Here they are, individually and idiosyncratically told.

Quality

Definitions:

Quality as a person, and quality of life.

The best, highest standard.

How well you do something, or bring out qualities in other people.

Parents act as role models, and so they can promote good qualities. This means praising the qualities of the family as a whole and individually; talking about or reflecting upon qualities of life; finding ways of bringing out positive qualities in themselves, and stimulating their children in this way; and noticing how well the family or its individual members do something.

An understanding of quality would encompass other values, among them understanding, truth, love, friendship, compassion and humility.

Unity

Parents could recall an occasion when there was a family row or disagreement. How did everyone feel? Was it a happy feeling? Discussion about how the situation was resolved and comparison of the feelings involved (unhappy-disturbing/happy-united) would be helpful and constructive. A family as a group is happiest when united.

Peace

Peace is freedom from conflict, both inside ourselves and in the wider world. You could talk about your own ideas of peace, and your children's. You could talk about peace of mind. Encourage your children to discuss their worries. How can they resolve them? If any worries have arisen because of actions or words causing unhappiness to others, *always* try to set it right. This goes for parents as well as children.

Take the idea of peace within the family further out, into the community, the country and the world. Each individual can be tolerant and forgiving towards others. Always try to resolve conflict peacefully and be prepared to negotiate – it doesn't matter if you lose face. And never let the sun go down on your wrath.

Happiness

As a family, discuss the things that make you happy. What has mum, dad, sister, brother done today/this week to make you feel happy? Can we decide to feel happy, or do we need to have an obvious reason? When we are sad, can we acknowledge it and dispel it, or perhaps tell someone close to us about it and then move on? Do we do anything to make others happy? If we do, is it because it makes us happy or because we are expecting a reward?

Happiness is a good feeling. It can be temporary if sought from external sources, such as wealth, status and relationships. Lasting happiness is a state of contentment within, not needing to be fed by outside wants.

At home perhaps you'd like to:

Find a quiet time such as bed-time when the family can share their happy thoughts.

When the family is together, perhaps during a meal, each member can tell what makes them feel happy. The family can then try to ensure that everyone can have a happy time.

Another time, each person tells of some way they can make someone else happy, or some way they have already done so.

Hope

As a family, discuss what you hope will happen in the future. Good times for this might be the New Year, when you could decide on a hope as a family and follow it through the next twelve months. Or discuss the meaning of hope at the birthdays of family members, when the person having the birthday could decide on their aspirations and the family could consider how they could support them.

Patience

This is about being patient with others and with yourself when things don't happen as you would like. Try complimenting members of your family:

When they have waited patiently for their turn when food is being dished up.

For not seeing their favourite television programme because someone else wanted to watch another channel.

For giving others the chance to speak first.

Talk about what the word means and how members of the family show it. You might tell the children about times when you have had to be patient, perhaps waiting in a queue. Describe how hard it is to be patient when you're hungry or desperately keen to do something. Showing patience requires inner discipline – how do you develop it?

For younger children, have a chart at home on which you draw a happy face every time each child shows patience. Show your child that you notice and appreciate it when s/he displays patience. Draw your child's attention to anyone else who shows patience. Remember a time when someone lost their temper. As a family think of three strategies that could have helped you keep your temper.

Caring

The notion of caring can come into children's lives from quite early, when they see how we care for pets or plants. When they are old enough, children can be given such responsibilities themselves. You can also point out the ways in which family members care for each other, the things you do, how you show, for example, sympathy or support.

As a family you can talk about how you care for each other.

Loving each other constantly.

Putting other members of the family first.

Giving up time for each other.

Being patient.

Ask the children to talk about how they care for other members of the family. Talk about how the family can show more care – perhaps by being more thoughtful or helpful, or by doing things to help without being asked.

Humility

Discuss how humility is about not showing-off. Encourage your children to do something without needing to be praised for it. Make one day a week (to begin with) when each member of the family does something for someone else, to experience the good feeling you get from being selfless.

Simplicity

A beautiful word, and one that is a particular pleasure to define. Everything simple has quality, most simple things are forgotten or dismissed by the materialistic world. When you ask five-year-olds what they like best, they answer: 'my mum,' 'my dad,' 'a cuddle,' or 'a good night story'. These are all simple things that do not cost money. When you become older and more sophisticated it is often the simplest things that give the greatest pleasure: a fine day, a song, the early morning light in the garden. As a family you could talk about the word and what it means to you. You might like to notice that your favourite things are also simple, for example:

Bicycle rides.

Walks in the park.

Preparing a simple meal – the joy of doing something for someone else.

Time with your family free of computers, television etc.

Trust

Find a job for your child or children to do and then trust them to do it. Evaluate what happened and talk about it. Were they trustworthy? If so, they naturally deserve praise. Are you trustworthy? Are there some areas in which you can be trusted and others where you cannot (some people can be counted on to be late)? Who do they trust? Is there anyone they do not trust? What has brought that about?

Freedom

Talk about what freedom is: who has it, who has not. Talk about what each member of the family has the freedom to do and why the freedoms are different. This implies talking about different responsibilities. Decide together to give your child the freedom to do or choose something for the first time – after discussing the responsibility involved in it.

In all the examples, first seek understanding of the value through discussion, then reflect on it and think how it applies in your life, and lastly find some way of showing the value through your actions.

Another note on freedom comes from *West Kidlington Dolphin News* (the newsletter for parents): 'Freedom is something that in this country we take for granted and it is helpful to remind the children that it is a word that can be misunderstood. It does not give us permission to do what we like when we like! Full freedom functions only when rights are balanced with responsibilities and choice is balanced with conscience.'

Co-operation

Family life is co-operative. You can explain to your family how as parents you help each other, and for example how you can all work together when a new baby arrives. A child should enter an environment of co-operation and see their mum and dad working together. Children should always be praised for helping, for tidying up, being thoughtful and so on. They should also be praised for brushing their teeth, getting dressed and similar everyday tasks.

Each child needs to be praised for their individual efforts and qualities and siblings should be praised together when they co-operate in ways like these: sharing toys, respecting each other's space and time, accepting each other's need for peace and quiet, helping each other, helping around the house.

Understanding

Children are more likely to understand others if they experience being understood themselves. Parents can ensure that there is some prime time every day, perhaps after a meal or before going to bed, when the child knows that the parents' attention is fully focused on them. This will help children to experience being listened to and making sense of the world in the company of a listening adult.

Family life can be very hectic! Children know this, intuitively keeping tabs on their parents' moods. This is another reason why it is worth establishing a regular time for reflection and listening to your child. Your child will grow to value and enjoy these times, and to associate understanding with close, attentive listening.

Honesty

Have a family discussion to look at this word. You could ask everyone:

How do we feel when someone has lied to us?

Have we ever borrowed something and not returned it?

Should we cheat when playing games?

There are plenty of folk stories that illustrate the significance of honesty. The boy who cried wolf once too often is among the best-known, and has a modern counterpart in the story mentioned in Chapter Four: Matilda who cried 'fire!' untruthfully, and finally was not believed but burned to death instead. It is not hard to draw the conclusion that honesty is the best policy.

Appreciation

Talk about how the word means noticing and usually commenting on something good that has happened or been done for you, or something attractive that has been made. Point out how much people enjoy being appreciated, or having their work appreciated. At the end of a play you show your appreciation by clapping – how else do you show appreciation? Let all the family members say something they appreciate about all the others.

Courage

Emphasise to your children that it's OK to feel afraid. Courage is being afraid but still doing what you feel to be the right thing. You can talk to them about stories in which people have shown courage. Dorothy in *The Wizard of Oz* and Tiny Tim in *A Christmas Carol* are two of the best-known examples of fictional characters who had to overcome fear and still do the necessary deeds. If you are afraid about anything (or just nervous, anxious or apprehensive), you might talk to other parents and caring adults about it. They might suggest strategies for coping.

Love
You could talk about how love is always there, even when you are cross with each other. Talk about all the different kinds of love. You can show how love does not have to be romantic and is not possessive. Love is an aspect of pure giving and does not ask for any return: unconditional love is the most difficult kind for us to aspire to and the purest. A useful story book is *Dogger* by Shirley Hughes.

Friendship
Talk to your child about what friendship means, and find a practical example. After your child's friend has visited your house, ask what qualities the friend has that make your child feel friendly towards them. These might be the physical manifestations of friendship: hugging, smiling, handshaking, kissing, eye contact and so on (within reason!). The signs of friendship are all open. They are not crossed arms or closed language.

You could also talk about the sort of words your children's friends use that show friendship, and the sort of things they do together, and the things they do for each other. How do they answer the question, 'Who is my friend?' (An account of a discussion with five- and six-year-olds on this subject is given in Chapter Three.)

Thoughtfulness
Talk about what actions are considered to be thoughtful. Every morning for a week, decide on someone you will try to show thoughtfulness to, either by saying something to them or doing something for them. Talk about how it made you and the other person feel afterwards. Try being thoughtful for someone you do not particularly like and see if you can see their point of view even if you do not agree with it. Notice how doing that changes your perception of that person.

Tolerance
Discuss tolerance with your child, relating it to relationships with brothers

and sisters. In discussion, invite your children to describe three things they like about their brother/sister, and one thing they have difficulty living with. Ask how it makes them feel. Talk about accepting one another, including faults, and praise them when they show tolerance.

Responsibility

Giving children responsibility is one of the most caring things you can do and an essential part of their development. At West Kidlington School they participate in ways such as monitoring the playground and running the office at lunchtime, tasks for which there are always more volunteers than vacancies. They talk about it afterwards, even at secondary school, and say how much they enjoyed it.

When you give responsibility you should support it but not take it over. You could consider responsibilities such as:

- Looking after a pet
- Shopping for mum and dad
- Waking up and going to bed independently
- Tidying the bedroom regularly
- Earning pocket money.

The perception of responsibility as something shared within the family community, to each according to their abilities, is a useful one to clarify.

Respect

Talk to your children about different aspects of respect, for example in behaviour, in their manners, when showing qualities such as tolerance, patience and caring, and when thinking about other people before yourself. Also notice how people gain respect. They may gain it from their behaviour, from the way they treat other people, or simply from their position in society.

During the early stages of the positive values programme, the teachers made many assessments of how it was changing their own outlook and that of the children. Linda Heppenstall offered this success story.

'A girl in my class with visual and motor skills impairment, from a poor economic and social background, was seen at the start of the year as someone different. Because of this she was often ridiculed and isolated by the other children.

'As I write, we have just returned from a games lesson where she was chosen by a team leader for her rounders team even though her problems mean that she cannot help them win. She was encouraged and praised throughout by many of the class and afterwards she said, "I enjoyed that, Mrs Heppenstall!"

'The look on her face said it all. The whole class has made great progress in understanding, and she is one of them.'

Living the values

Take the value words one by one and try them out for a week, a fortnight or a month at a time (but be consistent). With your children, make a big poster of the word and put it up in your hall or kitchen. If the children are old enough, let them make it themselves. Use it as a constant reminder, let it make you smile and remind you of your current effort – but never use it as a stick to beat people with. During the period of your value word, let parents give one example of how you show respect/trust/love/word of choice. In return, your children could describe how they show that value. These could be recorded in a Family Values book.

These are beautiful ideals to aspire to. There should be no coercion, only the joy that comes from working together and admitting that you are having to try as hard as they are. The fact that the understanding is subtle and the work is gentle increases their strength.

There is something fundamental about a common understanding that goes much deeper than simply a common language. If one considers how differently American and British people think, using the same words, you can see that the same applies by extension within Britain. All words are understood slightly differently by everyone who uses them and this applies much more to important abstract concept words. Several West Kidlington parents reported in Chapter Seven that their children's definitions of the positive values often brought them up short. We may think we all have the same idea of a word such as *trust* but find that our associations with and interpretations of it vary greatly. Discussion will bring out interesting points of view, interesting stories, and the very act of discussion will not only make us exercise our brains but also imprint positive ideas on sub-conscious minds. Precision with language needs to be encouraged. Like organic food, it requires more effort and is infinitely better for us.

With time and effort, the depth of understanding of the meanings of the positive value words will grow, like a well-watered garden. You can't rush it. You can reflect on it, consider it, observe it – and, like the children at West Kidlington School, let it take root in your sub-conscious so that it becomes not only part of your outward behaviour but an essential part of your inner being and the way you look at the world. Be amazed: the world is a brighter and more beautiful place when looked at through the lens of positive appraisal instead of the conventional one of criticism. Appraisal does not make judgements but weighs up situations quietly and determines upon positive action. Appraisal deals in good solutions.

More good solutions

There are anxieties common to most parents of school-age children, and some troubles that mercifully affect only a few. This section is about transformations. Of course, the best and most loving solutions come when you create a home life in which everybody knows their roles, a culture based on openness and respect. This will include much talking, and will exclude judgement-making or wanting to change people. In such an atmosphere there will be few troubles and those there are will be soon dispersed.

Conversations are important, undertaken in the right spirit and at the right time. Try to find times to talk when you aren't too tired. Tiredness clouds your mind and affects your emotional state so that you are more likely to react, instead of responding in a considered way. In conversations about how things are to be, or how they might have gone better, it is important to ensure that everybody wins.

If anyone walks out of the room thinking they have lost, you are storing up trouble for later; at some point their resentment will find expression. This is summarised: *you can't win an argument*, so be careful that everyone goes away with something positive. For parents wanting a conversation with a teacher the same principles apply: wait until you are calm.

The most common troubles are broadly: bullying, confidence (social or academic), quality of academic and personal effort and domestic tragedy. When such troubles are brought to Mr. Hawkes he receives them in this spirit:

- Listening dispassionately and kindly.

- Being non-judgmental.

- Being flexible in attitude (not school-masterish).

- Being honest – saying how it is (but mercifully).

- Remaining calm and having positive feelings.

- Not harbouring bad feelings even when people are unjustly critical.

- Being human, not appearing never to have had problems.

- Having a sense of humour.

- Ensuring that my own position/values are understood.

- Maintaining confidentiality. This is *vital*: then parents know you have integrity and they trust you.

- Not saying things just to be popular.

- Being consistent in morale and manner – there are no bad days to see the head teacher.

- Following a conversation with a note or a telephone call, when a parent, a teacher or a child is having difficulty.

- Showing that you are unbiased and objective, and not just protecting your staff.

- Showing that you genuinely care about people.

Many of these qualities could be useful to parents and of them, listening without judgement is paramount. Objectivity means that when parents take the problem to school they are not defensive but see it as a home/school issue in which everyone can support everyone else. They can go with an open, uncritical attitude, and not set up a meeting just for the sake of having a go at members of staff.

It is worth writing down the points of discussion so that the school knows them in advance of the visit – and writing them not in the way of just telling tales but emphasising that you want to help the child. Ensure that you are seeing the right person, who will almost certainly be your child's teacher. Only go to someone else if the teacher cannot handle the problem, and don't go over their head unless you absolutely have to.

Have your meeting in the spirit of, 'what can we do about this together?' Make it clear that you want action – but mutual action. Never be afraid to be assertive, but beware of speaking about the problem in front of the child to another adult in such a way as to imply that the school is wrong (even if you think it is). This implies a lack of confidence, which the child will absorb and find disturbing. When you get to the meeting, be prepared to be open about your child, then you may solve the problem together.

Bullying

With questions of bullying, a common observation is that the child who is on the receiving end of it may in some way be attracting it. This may sound strange, but we have to wonder why else some of the children who are mild, unconventional non-joiners avoid being got at, and others seem almost to be automatic targets.

When your child brings home tales of bullying, listen dispassionately and don't jump to conclusions. Children view their lives from a limited perspective and are not aware of their own input into situations. They think everything that is done, is done *to* them. They tell their story from that point of view and they usually conclude by asking you to go to school and sort it out. Ask the school policy on bullying, ask for advice and help on ways of handling it.

Before you go to school, ask yourself some questions. Is my child happy at home? Does my child participate in clubs or social situations? What activities do I do with my child? Do we go out together, or with friends? Do we as parents argue in front of our child? Next, consider the context of the bullying incidents. Ask this, why is my child going to school and acting as a victim?

Part of the solution is to enable the child to strengthen his or her inner self. It is no good trying tactics of bravado or showing-off, these are only displays and will be spotted at once and attract more trouble. It is also no good them trying to meet force with force: the bullied child will be outflanked by superior strength or numbers.

Instead, parents of children who are being bullied need to give them coping strategies. The practice of reviewing the day and reflecting on the consequences of actions will help to bring fresh thoughts on how it could have gone better. Was the bullied child perhaps calling people names, bossing them, or trying to be superior? Might such tactics have been avoided?

Children who are sure of themselves from the inside can be as eccentric as they like and still be left alone. They need to take stock of their positive qualities and use them. They may need to have their positive qualities pointed out and reinforced. Another idea is to learn a peaceful, non-combative physical discipline such as judo. It brings extra confidence and has the paradoxical advantage that those who have the skill rarely need to use it. Neil Hawkes believes that 99 per cent of bullying can be prevented in one way or another by the person/child who is being bullied. People who have genuine self-esteem rarely attract bullying.

Social confidence

For social confidence problems it can be helpful to bring parents into the classroom, as happened with Stephen Killick (see Chapter Seven). It does not matter if the parent is not directly involved with teaching his or her shy child, the simple fact of their presence in the classroom or even just in the school building can stabilise a child who is over-sensitive or jittery. There is also much to be gained from gently asking the child's opinions, getting them to express their wishes, say what they like and don't like. When to cover for them and when to encourage them to speak for themselves is a difficult question. Claire Killick found she had been over-protecting her son somewhat, which quite often happens. The golden rule here, as so often with children, is *ask them sensitively what you can do to help them*. Then don't just leave it there, put it into action.

Lack of confidence with school work

This is another common worry. Confidence coupled with determination and perseverance can make a huge difference to the success of even an academically average child. Here again, the calm state in which the child embarks on a task that he or she finds difficult will affect its outcome. The mind when it is overwound or panicky cannot take in very much; a nervous child can become like a rabbit in the headlights of a car, practically unable to do anything. Deep breathing, inner calm, gentle, strong encouragement and a spirit of determination and belief in possibility will bring academic rewards. It will help not only the activity of doing the work but also the ability of the child to ask clear questions about what he or she does not understand.

Exceptional children

The question of the exceptional child has some parallels with the unconfident problem. Many parents believe their child is extra-special and of course they are right, all children are. But some children are indeed very different, either specially gifted or in some way academically disadvantaged. Parents do not know the extent to which schools make provision for this and at West Kidlington the teachers often have to explain how much serious consideration is given to the needs and abilities of each individual child. Their assessment is made on the basis of evidence from teachers and learning support assistants, and not just on someone's general feeling.

Very gifted children are usually the children of academically able parents, who nearly always want their child moved up. At the school they explain the sophisticated sequence of observation that goes into deciding where each child is best placed. Neil Hawkes says, 'We don't stick rigidly to keeping them in an age group. There may be a case for a child being in another class for part of the time but not all of it. Often parents who are academically successful find these questions difficult because they don't understand how a primary school works. They've either forgotten, or they remember an outdated version, and they make assumptions about work that are not accurate, for example that the curriculum for a particular year group is rigidly stuck to and therefore their child won't be stretched.

'They don't know that teachers are always aiming to extend each child, and materials from different year groups are used to do it. With an IQ spread of between 75 and 130 you couldn't be using the same materials for all pupils in a year group – but the school has always to ask whether the child's interests would be best served in a group of children who are older. We then move into questions of different kinds of intelligence, interpersonal skills and so on, and we ask whether the child is socially and emotionally able to be in a group that is physically older. A great deal of care and trouble is taken by all the staff before any interview with parents. In any case of this kind, I will see the child and the child's work, so that I can assure parents that any decision is based on evidence.' Such a detailed study is likely to take place in all schools.

Special Needs is a category that includes a broad spread of learning difficulties. These problems are supported by a range of special provisions and learning support but at West Kidlington they are supported uniquely by the values programme. Neil Hawkes says, 'By emphasising the positive and raising each child's self-esteem the programme actively creates success, because children with learning difficulties do not perceive themselves as being in some way different and not quite up to the mark. Their relationship with their teachers is very good (as with all the children) and the ethos of the school says that children have different capabilities and skills, all of which are to be celebrated. Each child has something special: it might be a lovely smile, or the ability always to say the right thing to someone who is distressed – or they may be a good swimmer, or someone who makes peace in the playground. Because we celebrate all those qualities children with difficulties can thrive in a way that is qualitatively different, and reach their optimum potential.'

Domestic tragedy

Of the many varieties, marriage breakdown is probably the most common. There are also large general headings: bereavement; favourite relations moving away or having rows; family explosions over Wills or division of property; families not being able to cope, and many variations.

Within this range of distressing events the common element is loss. Support your child/children emotionally as much as you possibly can. Talk about the trouble, let them cry if they need to (although your sensitivity and discretion must see when crying is becoming an end in itself), put up with it when they direct their anger at you. If you are upset let them see it, but let them also see that you are strong enough to sustain them through the disaster. They must not get the terrifying impression that they are cut loose from a solid anchor, because that can leave dreadful scars.

In the case of a death, talk about the person who has gone, their delightful characteristics and the fun you had together. At West Kidlington, the staff are able to support children who have lost family members including siblings, who are among the most distressing losses. Such a bereavement happened to one of the ten-year-olds when she was six, and in the Infants class. It affected both her and her mother very deeply, and they grieved together. Nothing was hidden, nothing swept under the carpet, and all the teachers were available to listen and support the whole family. From time to time they still talk about it even now. Grieving has no set time-scale.

Neil Hawkes believes that for the home/school relationship to have integrity, the school community needs to be interested in home circumstances and events and the home community needs to be open with the school. 'A school needs to see its responsibility far wider,' he says. 'We need a different concept, of a school as a common resource for the education of the whole community. If we have the trust of the community there can be help on a huge scale, and growth through openness. We need a no-blame culture. There are always mistakes, there are always things that create worry and anxiety – but most things in most schools can be sorted out. One of the myths we need to get rid of is that all adults are intelligent, balanced and capable – in fact there is a range of abilities among adults just as much as there is among children. Parents need support. They might be prepared to say, "We don't know what to do" – then we could make some progress.'

In common with all schools, West Kidlington has to contend with the consequences of divorce and the re-establishment of new families. The school is then servicing the old set of parents and the new ones, and among the logistical consequences of this is the fact that they have to send scores of newsletters to parents who do not live with their children, just to keep them in the picture.

The critically important thing in such situations is to avoid making the child feel responsible. Of course, they never are, but they think they are, and it can be devastating to them. Make sure the child feels loved by all the adults around them; make sure they know that both parents love them and that their love will remain constant. The two most terrible distresses experienced by children over parental relationship problems are these: feeling responsible, and feeling that one of the parents doesn't love them.

If you have fallen out, do not have rows in front of the children. Children find it difficult to understand what is going on. They love both the parties and don't know where to place their loyalty. Re-focus and take a different approach with your partner, one that puts the children first. Have the self-discipline to make proper visiting arrangements and keep to them as civilly as possible. Do not use your children as pawns or battering-rams in your own cause, it is outrageously irresponsible and will practically guarantee that their own future relationships are doomed also. As always, a shared belief in universal values is important.

Big rewards

Just as the happy, balanced, hard-working, well-mannered children of West Kidlington Primary School receive no national certificates for their demeanour, their behaviour and positive contribution to their communities, so it is with adults. There is no tangible or measurable gain. You are not promised status or money. You are not promised greater popularity (although you may find it) or a visible make-over (although as you become calmer and more fulfilled you may become more beautiful). Another difference between this work and more mundane types is that you do not reach a point of saying, 'I've got there!' It is a continuing task, year in and year out, just like doing the garden, and similarly the rewards are constant.

The word spiritual is re-entering the popular vocabulary in a peculiar way: it is currently being used to advertise commercial products including a classical CD and an eye-shadow. It has been used sparingly in this book but it should be clear that the values work is attempting to enable the children and adults who take part in it to reach their highest selves. This access will be available at all times and will be most noticeably helpful in emotional crises or situations when people need to make difficult decisions about proper action. The use and examination of the positive value words is proposed because it has appeal for all religious faiths and none, it is a rock upon which character, behaviour, outlook, learning and happiness can be built. It is a means towards reaching the inner world which has been so catastrophically neglected by the material, lifestyle culture, and it is the route to real fulfilment and understanding.

And now it's your turn ...

Appendix

Ahead of one of their Ofsted inspections, the staff at West Kidlington Primary School were asked to show how Spiritual, Moral, Social and Cultural considerations influenced the teaching of all their subjects. This exercise offers another illustration of the comprehensive nature of the values programme. Although the programme is based on one or two very simple ideas, its realisation is deep, complex and far-reaching.

Just as the positive concepts can permeate the teaching of virtually all class subjects, so subtly and carefully they can enter home life. Such continuity is immensely reassuring and strengthening to children. It gives them a strong framework from which to view the world and find their place in it. And, of course, it provides just such a healthy forward-looking framework for parents too. The constant reiteration of the positive is a matchless tonic for perception and attitude.

SPIRITUAL

ENGLISH	Literature, including story and poetry that explores human experience and response to life and death. Use of stillness and imagination in drama and other activities to develop inner awareness. Expressing feelings and emotions through verbal and written communication knowing that words can influence feelings.
MATHS	Enjoyment and fascination of numbers, including the idea of infinity. Reflecting on pattern and order, as well as a sense of mystery and space. Exploring the relationships of numbers, shapes and objects and the possibility of inter-connectedness. Sense of achievement and self-worth at appropriate levels of understanding.
SCIENCE	Scientific links with a spiritual interpretation about universe and life. Using the school grounds for reflection on relationships between people and their environment. Reflecting on the mystery of the natural world and physical worth, life cycles and growth. Awareness of physical self as wonderful.
TECHNOLOGY	Sense of worth in human potential and achievement. Designing cards for religious festivals. Making holy books and other artefacts/special objects.
IT	Through the internet, connectedness with people all over the world. Using programmes to create poems and pictures. Becoming independent and developing self-reliance.

HISTORY	Ideas of change and development and re-creation. Understanding of the importance of tradition to a community. Sense of time and awareness of personal place within it.
GEOGRAPHY	How things came about, and a sense of wonder at the earth's variety and order. Developing self-awareness and relationships with other cultures and environments. Appreciation of natural features e.g. lakes, woods.
ART	Idea of beauty in art. Appreciation of colour and shape and texture. Religious and spiritual ideas expressed in, e.g. stained glass windows. Art as a means of expressing feelings, imagination and creative thought.
MUSIC	Making music by singing together, songs and hymns and with instruments. Listening to specific chosen pieces, and why people write music e.g. Hallelujah chorus. Identifying feelings and emotions associated with different types of music. Using music as a background to times of quiet and reflection to develop awareness of the inner self.
RELIGIOUS EDUCATION	Knowledge of religious reflection and spiritual practices e.g. worship. Providing opportunities for experiencing space and silence to allow skills in reflection and awareness to develop. Meeting others who belong to other traditions. Providing opportunities for experiencing awe, wonder and transcendence.
PHYSICAL. EDUCATION	Spiritual awareness of body, its beauty and potential, through activity and observation. Movement to express feelings and emotions including dancing for joy. Developing inner determination to do one's best and recognise and develop one's inner potential and strength.

SOCIAL

ENGLISH	Circle time skills in speaking and listening. Social interaction through play. Writing and communicating with an audience. Group drama work, reading and discussion of social issues in literature. Stories to create awareness of a variety of life experiences e.g. deafness.
MATHS	Maths games for social interaction, taking turns and sharing. Working in pairs and groups to gather information and solve problems. Recognising maths skills as a tool for society.
SCIENCE	Investigation in groups sharing expertise and skills. Science as a co-operative activity requiring communication and interaction. Science related to issues in society e.g. alcohol abuse.
TECHNOLOGY	Designing with others. Using technology to benefit others e.g. handicapped.
IT	Working co-operatively. Using data handling skills to promote understanding of social issues. Poster design for safety.
HISTORY	Exploring structures of society, including institutions, e.g. hospice, hospital, work house. Looking at children past and present. Understanding the influence of the past on the development of society today.

GEOGRAPHY	Local studies to raise awareness of different homes, communities and family groupings. Local amenities: who are they for? Human influence e.g. Tourism on island of St Lucia, Caribbean. Group fieldwork opportunities.
ART	Art as a means of learning about people and society. Group collage e.g. creating murals.
MUSIC	Taking part in a performing arts activities, e.g. school assembly/pantomime. Collaborative work and sharing resources, e.g. instruments, taking turns. Group singing and composition.
RELIGIOUS EDUCATION	Knowing about and understanding the importance of family and traditions within religious faiths. Study of ideas of community in religions. Researching charities and other religious forms of social caring and responsibility.
PHYSICAL EDUCATION	Participation in traditional and creative dance and pair and group work in gymnastics. Enjoyment of team games, showing co-operation, respect for others and their needs. Participation and observation as social skills.

MORAL

ENGLISH	Discussion of right and wrong – moral issues exemplified in children's literature. Skills of listening and forming evaluative judgements in discussion. Circle time discussion of behaviour and relationships. Dramatising situations which raise moral questions.
MATHS	Encouraging a sense of personal responsibility for their own learning in class and through homework. Encouraging honesty, not cheating. Awareness of manipulation of data (statistics).
SCIENCE	Thinking about experiments and investigations and their outcomes for humans. Caring for living things e.g. classroom guinea pig, plant. Discussing issues raised by scientific discovery and progress e.g. cloning, genetic engineering, travel in space.
TECHNOLOGY	Learning co-operation with others through activities. Technology as helpful and constructive as well as potentially destructive.
IT	Independent working to develop a sense of integrity and trustworthiness. Discussion of moral issues e.g. correct information, pornography.
HISTORY	Developing awareness of local, national, world issues. Encounter with ideas and encouragement to think through a moral stance on issues e.g. war and peace. Stories to illustrate changes in attitudes.

GEOGRAPHY	Developing moral responsibility to care for environment e.g. farming and hedgerows. Awareness of human exploitation e.g. child labour in developing countries. Poverty amidst affluence. Awareness of misuse of earth's resources and human responses e.g. recycling and deforestation.
ART	Interpreting pictures which put a moral point of view.
MUSIC	Appreciation of music and respecting the ideas and judgements of others. Learning about and from the lives of musicians.
RELIGIOUS EDUCATION	Stories with a moral message from world religions. Ideas of right and wrong behaviour in world religions. Individual and corporate responsibility within religious communities. Developing skills of listening, respecting and evaluative judging.
PHYSICAL EDUCATION	Taking part in team games and obeying rules. Awareness of others' needs, particularly physical. Encouragement to cheer, celebrate achievement and shake hands at end of a game. Developing a sense of fair play, not hurting anyone

CULTURAL

ENGLISH	Stories and literature from other cultures. Awareness of issues such as stereotyping and equal opportunities in literature. Language and meanings in different cultures.
MATHS	Creating Islamic patterns, rangoli patterns and using Roman Numerals. Careful choices of resources and examples to include references to other cultures. Shopping in a multicultural area. Counting in a different language.
SCIENCE	Differences and similarities between groups of humans. Animals from different countries. Creation stories from different cultures alongside current scientific stories. Role of science in different cultures and religions. Scientific development in relation to others – water supplies, new varieties of flowers and food crops.
TECHNOLOGY	The effectiveness of very simple technology in some cultures. Instruments from different countries, e.g. cooking utensils. Designs for different climates e.g. sun hats.
IT	Accessing information about cultures by using CD-ROMs, etc. Direct contact with children in other cultures through world wide web and e-mail. Making an Islamic pattern.

HISTORY	The story of development of a variety of cultures. Stories of religious leaders and their influence on cultures. History of contribution of other cultures to science and maths.
GEOGRAPHY	Study of people – especially children living in different countries and comparisons with own cultural context. Developing an awareness and appreciation of different styles of everyday life. The influence of environment on societies.
ART	Pictures from different cultures, e.g. African art. Visiting exhibitions and art galleries to view art from different cultures. Art as expression of a culture e.g. Nativity pictures on Christmas cards.
MUSIC	Music from different cultures e.g. Calypso songs from the Caribbean. Listening to and using instruments from other cultures.
RELIGIOUS EDUCATION	The study of different religions as part of a cultural tradition. Meeting people from a variety of faiths and cultures and visiting places of worship. Exploring how religious ideas are expressed in different cultures e.g. food, dress, patterns festivals and celebrations.
PHYSICAL EDUCATION	Dance as an expression of culture e.g. Indian Folk. Teams adopting names of international sides.

(see also http://atschool.eduweb.co.uk/west.kidlington)